T0350799

TRUMP
AND
REAGAN

TRUMP
AND
REAGAN

DEFENDERS OF AMERICA

NICK ADAMS

Post Hill
PRESS

A POST HILL PRESS BOOK
ISBN: 978-1-64293-770-1
ISBN (eBook): 978-1-64293-771-8

Post Hill Press
New York • Nashville
posthillpress.com

Published in the United States of America
1 2 3 4 5 6 7 8 9 10

To all the people that have ever supported me.

CONTENTS

AUTHOR'S NOTE

At the time of this book going to print, a vaccine for COVID-19 under the leadership of President Trump has just been announced.

It remains unclear whether President Trump will win another four years in the White House.

What is clear?

That even if President Trump is not re-elected, he will have achieved more in one term than President Reagan did in two.

And President Ronald Reagan was pretty spectacular.

President Trump's legacy as the most consequential president since Abraham Lincoln is cemented.

The forty-fifth president—Donald J. Trump—is our greatest modern-day president.

PREFACE

It is March 2, 2016.

I've just stepped off the set of *Lou Dobbs Tonight* on the Fox Business channel, doing Super Tuesday election coverage.

With only a few results in, I have just predicted not only that Donald Trump will win the nomination, but that he will also win the presidency in November.

My phone begins to light up.

"Did you really just predict live on air that Trump will win the whole thing?!"

"Did you just say what I thought you did?!"

"Dude, you jumped the gun. Big-time!"

Even Lou looked a little startled at the certainty with which I delivered the following words:

"I think it's very clear that Donald Trump is going to be the next president of the United States. I think he's going to absolutely pulverize Hillary Clinton in a general election. I think he's going to wrap up this nomination very quickly…"

Lou stammered, "Well, it doesn't…that isn't what is reflected in the head-to-head polling, though, as you know, Nick…"

And then promptly changed the topic!

The truth is, I always knew Donald Trump was going to become president.

Call it a gut instinct.

Even while still living in Australia in 2011, I was disappointed when he dropped out of the 2012 Republican primary race in the U.S., because I felt the anodyne, flavorless, and, as it turns out, insanely jealous and horrible hypocrite Mitt Romney clearly didn't have it in him.

Instead, we got stuck with four more years of the weakest and most divisive president ever, and America was pushed to the precipice.

In 2015, when Trump got in the race, I was all-in.

I knew that Trump's personality and style of leadership were perfect to reverse the Obama years. I knew that he was the new Reagan—with the potential to be even better.

As the campaign progressed, even from its earliest stages, I could see what was coming, and I called it. Often and publicly. Almost every one of my fellow commentators and pundits, as well as my friends, thought I was a sandwich short of a picnic.

When Trump placed second in the Iowa caucuses on February 1, 2016, I was even more certain of my Trump-Reagan comparison.

Reagan had placed second in Iowa too, in 1980.

The signs were good!

The year 2016 was big for me—it was the year that I finally immigrated to the United States. It was also an extraordinary year for the United States of America—a year when civilization got a reprieve and America got a chance to arrest its slide. Decline, after all, is a choice, not a condition.

Americans chose greatness once more.

President Trump has now endorsed three of my books while in office, over a series of ten tweets over three and a half years, prompting many people to very generously refer to me as "the president's favorite author."

I am beyond honored.

But the truth is that the president's shout-outs and support of my work began before he was even president.

My extremely early support for Donald Trump and supreme confidence in him did not go unnoticed.

Back in the mid-2010s, I was a columnist at the website Townhall, and on February 23, 2016, I wrote an article titled "Political Correctness—The Reason The World Needs To Use Its Trump Card." Here is the article in its entirety:

> Political correctness is destroying America, and Western civilization.
>
> This year America celebrates her 240th birthday. If she is to make her tri-centennial in 2076, a feat few great nations in history have achieved, it will need to crush this totalitarian ideology that is currently strangling it.
>
> Every problem in America today is linked to political correctness. Declining educational standards, increasing secularism, the police not being allowed to do their job, an inability to secure her borders, a diminished America in the world theatre and reluctance to smash the evil of currently rampaging Islamism—all of it is rooted in politically correct ideology. Nothing is more antithetical to America's foundational principles.
>
> Political correctness seeks to eliminate individualism, identity, and confidence; three characteristics indispensable to American greatness. If you want to see

the end result, look no further than Europe. The intellectual tyranny, self-loathing, and choking conformity of this ideology have feminized and weakened a once great continent which now aspires to mediocrity. The same is true of America's English-speaking cousins.

I write this not as an American.

But as somebody that wants Western civilization to prosper. Everyone has an investment in keeping the United States as culturally robust and powerful as imaginable, because the world's fortunes travel with it. What is good for America is good for the world.

I am here to tell you I've lived your future; if you keep going, you're not going to like it. It's why I've written "Retaking America: Crushing Political Correctness."

The entire world looks on as Americans make their choice for president. The president of the United States is also the president of the free world. All of us have a stake. For example, people in Australia aren't sleeping well right now because President Obama is not keeping the world safe. Change can't come quickly enough for many around the world.

The world needs an American president that is clear-minded and right-thinking. That encourages a climate of straight talking and decisive action. That has the moral clarity to defend Christians and the West. An alpha male prepared to win for his people.

People are losing their jobs, missing out on opportunities, and being targeted. What was born on college campuses has been armed through social media by electronic cockroaches that should never have been given a voice. The parameters of public debate have shrunk, and civil society's ability to conduct rational, cool-headed conversations is being usurped by a crude marketplace of outrage and a new victimhood movement. Freedom is an obvious casualty of political correctness, but following close behind is truth and reality.

Many people around the world despair. But every now and again, a public figure emerges who transcends politics and has an undisputed ability to change the culture.

This is why the world needs to use its Trump card. He is uniquely positioned to change the culture of the world, and restore American greatness and Western confidence through attitude alone.

A President Trump would be the best thing, not only for America, but for the entire world.

Proud, confident, bold, patriotic, outspoken, self-reliant, megasuccessful, charitable, a force of nature; Donald Trump is American exceptionalism on steroids.

For too long, America's educational and media elites have relentlessly and recklessly portrayed America as a hateful place. It's not. It's the greatest country in this history of the world. But political correctness is giving it an identity crisis. Some may well call Donald Trump an egomaniac and his election to the highest office risky—but right now, America needs an ego boost. It needs to believe in itself again. Only then can there be an American renaissance.

A Trump presidency won't only wipe out political correctness in America; it'll wipe it off the face of the earth.

This article caught the attention of then candidate Donald Trump, earning me my first promotion from him on social media, on February 24, 2016.

But it was my next article, on March 23, 2016, which he really liked, and that article set forth the motion of the book you're reading now. Titled "Trump Revolution Could Be More Incredible Than Reagan Revolution," here's the article in its entirety:

If Donald Trump becomes president, we may witness something more incredible than the Reagan Revolution.

The greatest modern-day president, Ronald Reagan, left an immensely powerful legacy. Almost three decades after his departure from the White House, he remains the conservative standard-bearer of the Republican Party.

Under his presidency, the United States witnessed a grand political realignment toward conservative foreign and domestic policies. Reagan's leadership boosted morale, confidence, patriotism, and America's economy and ended communism.

It has been difficult to conceive of a presidency that would trump the revolution of Reagan.

Until now.

Much is different, including the times, the threats, the challenges, and the world.

While it may have been unimaginable to generations of America that lived through the Carter years, America is in much worse shape than she was then.

Seven years of a president that has deliberately diminished America at home and abroad, in accordance with his worldview, beginning and ending with apology tours, have taken their toll.

Patriotism has become politically incorrect, and libeling America at will has become acceptable. Believing in American exceptionalism is now considered culturally obtuse, and academics at elementary, middle, and high schools, along with college campuses, intentionally and recklessly paint America as a hateful, bigoted, and oppressive place.

Political correctness, once born on college campuses, now weaponized by the leftist cockroaches that inhabit and preside over social media, has become a way of life. America is now in a race to become another European country, aspiring for mediocrity, resenting success, with all the self-loathing and suicidal inclinations we see in that continent.

There is a war on America. A war on Christians. A war on white, middle-class men and women. A war on anyone with traditional views on marriage, the environment, patriotism, and life. We lose our jobs. We miss out on opportunities. We're canceled as speakers or disinvited from social gatherings.

Enough is enough.

A President Trump would change that.

Every day ordinary people in America and around the world have been shunted and vilified from the mainstream. This is despite our moral and philosophical compass being common-sense conservatism.

Trump is going to give free-thinking conservatives the run of the table.

No more mainstream leftist censorship from social media.

No more political correctness for the sake of social engineering.

Just freedom.

This could be more incredible than the Reagan Revolution.

Imagine.

No more libeling of America.

God and patriotism back in schools.

Trump will reset the Obama presidency and its malefactors. Trump will transform the party to that of a coalition of blue-collar conservative workers and evangelicals Christians who want the U.S. to halt the war on Christianity.

A Trump presidency would be Culture War Ground Zero. With the disgraceful riots of Chicago a couple of weeks ago, Trump has emerged as the consensus leader against the left.

Many don't get it.

They don't get it that Trump is there to give them a leg up rather than be screwed over constantly by those who look down at them.

The Republican Establishment of today is the same as the Rockefeller crowd of the seventies.

As Brussels amply showed yesterday, the West is staring into the barrel here.

The Republicans in this millennium have only won the popular vote once. And that was by less than 1 percent. If they had a coalition of white conservatives voting for their own interests, they would win in landslides.

Like Reagan.

Reagan Democrats win landslides. Imagine making them a permanent fixture of the Republican voting base. The Democrats haven't changed one person's mind—they have changed the electorate instead.

As I have traveled throughout America, so many have told me: "Trump is our man." He's the guy, they say, that

has come to save the world from the path of self-destruc-
tion by the vices of our own virtues.

America needs to pull one for mankind, and seal this
one for Trump. For those who can't see it yet, the Trump
revolution will sweep them away.

On March 25, 2016, then candidate Donald Trump again
took to social media to share this article.

When I reread my words from almost five years ago, I am
just delighted at how accurate my predictions were.

It's hard to remember, given that the conservative world
is almost universally supportive and laudatory of the president now, but in March 2016, before Trump had even won the
primary, to suggest that he was going to have a greater, more
impactful, and consequential presidential legacy than Ronald
Reagan was considered insane.

Not to mention, it was considered offensive to Ronald
Reagan, even though that was not my intention.

I was born in September 1984, just two months before
Ronald Reagan crushed Walter Mondale in Reagan's reelection bid.

Sadly, I never got to meet President Reagan.

I remember being nineteen years old, in my second year of
college, and just beginning my political career when I learned
about his death.

Being a political nerd, I'm sure I knew a lot more about
Ronald Reagan than the average nineteen-year-old Australian.
But it wasn't until after his passing that I truly began to study
the fortieth president, reading every book and article I could
possibly get my hands on.

I discovered that Reagan was one of the greatest world leaders ever, and certainly the greatest modern-day president up until that point.

Of course, to reach that conclusion, I had to overcome the global media bias and the familiar fake-news narrative about President Reagan's lack of intellect.

In fact, the first thing I remember hearing about President Reagan while I was growing up was an account relayed by a former Australian prime minister Bob Hawke, which predictably led to the Australian mainstream media's casting unflattering opinions about Reagan's intelligence.

Here is one example:

> Reagan showed that not only could an actor become president but that you didn't even have to be a particularly good actor. As long as you stuck to the script and could sell a good line, all you needed to do was show up at the White House from nine to five, listen to people smarter than you and the country would pretty much run itself—which is precisely what Reagan did.
>
> Bob Hawke tells an insightful story about meeting the leader of the free world. Every time Hawke asked him a question, Reagan would answer in vague generalities or read points from a cue card. Then he would simply refer the PM to one of his cabinet secretaries or advisers for a proper response.[1]

Here's another snide dismissal of Reagan:

---

[1] https://www.dailytelegraph.com.au/news/opinion/joe-hildebrand-celebrity-apprentices-dont-add-up-to-real-leadership/news-story/af5f 01323a8c7f555e129acb871009df

Most astonishingly, Hawke discloses that Ronald Reagan, during meetings, read from cue-cards, producing generalised sentences on any subject raised by the visiting leader from a pack he kept in his hand.[2]

The media have never changed their tune, have they?

With my admiration for President Reagan sky high, throughout my journey toward America I always wondered if and when I would see another Ronald Reagan—a consequential president who would reshape the country and the Republican Party.

Comparisons are tough.

Different eras, different times, different circumstances, different competition—all make it difficult to determine the greatest of all time. We see it with sports debates. The same thing applies to presidents.

But in this case, the comparison I first made in early 2016, which has only solidified in my mind since, is spot-on.

Donald Trump is our new Reagan. And not to disrespect the greatness of Reagan at all, but I happen to think Trump is even better, and has been even more successful, and will leave an even greater legacy.

I do believe Trump is the GOAT (greatest of all time).

Clearly, Trump and Reagan are, at least on the surface, very different.

Reagan was genteel and almost never offended; Trump not so much. Reagan often carried a firearm and had a ranch for twenty-five years ("the Western White House"); Donald Trump

https://www.independent.co.uk/life-style/when-hawke-lets-fly-dream-up-a-tough-old-australian-with-the-full-vocab-and-youre-half-ready-for-bob-1446464.html is the product of America's biggest city, and a billionaire businessman. Reagan was avuncular and therefore more versatile in his presentation; Donald Trump is always the same—wearing a dark suit with a solid tie, and with that distinctive Queens accent. Reagan was unfailingly careful with his words; Trump is often impulsive.

But these two giants have an enormous amount in common:

- ▶ Both were around the same age when inaugurated.
- ▶ (Ronald Reagan was just a couple of weeks shy of his seventieth birthday when he was inaugurated. Donald Trump was just seven months older at the time of his inauguration, in January 2017.)
- ▶ Both were political outsiders, although of course, Donald Trump much more so than Ronald Reagan, with the former never having held any political office before being elected president.
- ▶ Their optimism and belief in American exceptionalism guided U.S. policies and activities—their ideology in many ways was American nationalism.
- ▶ Both were very much men of the 1980s and very "Hollywood."
- ▶ Both men possessed a very robust sense of personal and professional optimism and self-belief.
- ▶ Both were patriots who loved their country.
- ▶ They were the only two presidents to have been divorced.
- ▶ Both Reagan and Trump saw outer space as humanity's final frontier and as an opportunity for global leadership.

► Both endured battles with the political establishment, and both had the ability to speak over the media and directly to the people.

► Both were remarkable campaigners and gifted communicators.

► Both were charismatic and charming, with a sense of humor and color that enlarged their personalities, and both were convinced of the power of human agency. Neither man ever doubted his own capacity to persuade. They had an ability to identify the interests of the various players and bring them together in search of common ground.

► Many of the criticisms about both men were identical— that they were overly simplistic, were unintellectual, exploited white male resentments, and were devoid of nuance.

► Both were very pro-life, pro–Second Amendment, pro-military, pro-God presidents.

► Both cut regulations and taxes.

► Both relied heavily on private sector partnerships during their presidencies. (President Reagan created the Task Force on Private Sector Initiatives in 1981, and President Trump presided over a historic private sector partnership to combat COVID-19 in 2020)

► Both surrounded themselves with very successful self-made entrepreneurs and corporate chieftains, whom they appointed to Cabinet posts and high-level staff positions and advisory capacities.

The more I have researched this book, the more convinced I have become that Donald Trump is the second coming of Ronald Reagan.

What was visceral and predictive all those years ago when I penned that Townhall article is now indisputable and evidenced.

I predict that by the end of the Trump presidency, whether one or two terms, the annual major fundraisers held by county Republican parties across America will no longer be called Lincoln-Reagan Dinners or Reagan Day Dinners, but Trump-Reagan Dinners or Trump Day Dinners.

In the back of this book, you will find the best speeches of both President Reagan and President Trump. I highly recommend that you read them, reread them, and then read them aloud to your children. The next generation needs to know the words of the two very best modern-day American presidents.

In writing this book, I have drawn on nearly one hundred sources, including the writings of Trump, the writings of Reagan, biographers' books, contemporary writings, and the speeches of both men. I have used a diverse range of sources, including both conservative and liberal publications, attempting to use original source materials as much as possible. I have kept the source list at the end of this book simple but accessible. I am incredibly grateful for the work of the writers whose research and analysis I have drawn on for this book. Although primarily about President Trump and President Reagan, this book also is about the American people, the world, and the society we live in; therefore, it is part historical, part rallying cry, part sociological analysis. It is written for everyone but has Middle America, the heartland voter, the blue-collar Trump supporter in mind.

I hope you enjoy reading this book as much as I have enjoyed writing it.

INTRODUCTION

"[T]hey get bitter, they cling to guns or religion or antipathy toward people who aren't like them or anti-immigrant sentiment or anti-trade sentiment as a way to explain their frustrations."

—presidential candidate Barack
Hussein Obama in 2008, looking
down on Middle America[3]

"You know, to just be grossly generalistic, you could put half of Trump's supporters into what I call the basket of deplorables. Right? The racist, sexist, homophobic, xenophobic, Islamophobic—you name it. And unfortunately there are people like that. And he has lifted them up."

—failed presidential candidate
Hillary Clinton in 2016[4]

Why did I choose to start this book's introduction with quotes from two of our country's most anti-freedom, pro-globalism, pro–open borders Democratic politicians? To show you the contempt that people like Barack Hussein Obama

---

3   https://www.politico.com/blogs/ben-smith/2008/04/obama-on-small-town-pa-clinging-to-religion-guns-xenophobia-007737

4   https://time.com/4486502/hillary-clinton-basket-of-deplorables-transcript/

and Hillary Clinton have for people like you and me. And no doubt, they would have the same contempt for you if you were a Reagan supporter in 1980 as they have for you now as a supporter of President Trump in 2020. After all, the leadership and thought leaders of the Democratic Party, but not necessarily all of its members, at their core, despise you and me.

The core members of the Democratic Party, who were just as shocked when Reagan won in a massive landslide as when Trump upset Clinton in 2016, are motivated by disgust at American values. The core members of the Democratic Party are academics who get paid hundreds of thousands of dollars to spew anti-American hatred and to imbue in students a hatred of capitalism and American freedom, including freedom of speech, free enterprise, and the Second Amendment.[56]

Then there are, of course, the atheists and groups like the American Civil Liberties Union that want to drive religion, and particularly Christianity, out of the public square. Even a cross dedicated to veterans of war draws the ire of the lefties.[7]

There are, of course, the socialists who seek the destruction of America through government takeovers, open borders, and unlimited access to abortion and drugs. They do the work of the devil by seeking to undermine the bedrock of American society.

And, of course, there are the recent presidents and presidential candidates of the Democratic Party. Al Gore wants to tax Americans to death, and laid the groundwork for today's

---

[5] https://www.thecollegefix.com/economics-professor-blames-capitalism-for-americas-coronavirus-crisis/

[6] https://www.thecollegefix.com/professors-enthusiastically-tout-socialism-capitalism-course-sanders-youth-vote/

[7] https://www.nytimes.com/2019/06/20/us/politics/maryland-peace-cross-supreme-court.html

Green New Deal, which seeks nothing short of a complete shutdown of the American energy system. Pushed by hardcore communist Alexandria Ocasio-Cortez, the Green New Deal would decimate the American economy and put millions of people out of work. But when you're a Democratic leader, you just really do not care.

"American households can expect tens of thousands of dollars in higher costs for energy, housing, transportation, and shipping if the Green New Deal is implemented, according to a new study released today by Power the Future and the Competitive Enterprise Institute (CEI)," the Competitive Enterprise Institute reported.[8]

As the report noted, the GND calls for:

1. The elimination of "pollution and greenhouse gas emissions from the transportation sector as much as is technologically feasible";
2. "[U]pgrading all existing buildings in the United States and building new buildings to achieve maximal energy efficiency, water efficiency, safety, affordability, comfort, and durability, including through electrification";
3. "Where technologically feasible, the elimination of the use of fossil fuels and other combustible, greenhouse gas—emitting energy sources."

The costs would also be in the trillions: "Of interest for our analysis, [report authors Douglas] Holtz-Eakin and [Dan] Bosch estimate the costs of a 'low-carbon electricity grid' (at $5.4

---

[8] https://cei.org/content/what-green-new-deal-could-cost-typical-household

trillion versus Zycher's $8.95 trillion annual expenditures) as well as the costs of a zero-emission transportation system, and a national policy for 'green housing.'"[9]

And the Democratic Party also supports many terrible things that feed its lust to degrade human life. Consider that the party leadership supports unlimited abortions through all nine months of pregnancy, funded by taxpayers like you and me. And they want to force out pro-life Democrats.[10] Its top governors, like Andrew Cuomo and Ralph Northam, even believe that babies that survive abortion should be allowed to be killed through legalized infanticide.[11]

> The agenda pushed by New York Governor Andrew Cuomo and Virginia Governor Ralph Northam with regards to Planned Parenthood is unlimited abortion, on demand and at taxpayer expense. It also, evidently, involves targeting and attempting to silence people who are pro-life and doing the charitable work of reaching out to moms and babies in need.... [O]nly 7 percent of millennials agree with their unlimited abortion, on demand and at taxpayer expense agenda.[12]

Have you bought in now? The Democratic Party's leaders, but not necessarily rank-and-file Democrats, are enemies of freedom.

9 https://www.americanactionforum.org/research/the-green-new-deal-scope-scale-and-implications/
10 https://twitter.com/kristanhawkins/status/1217513801173667840
11 https://www.courier-journal.com/story/opinion/2019/02/04/ralph-northam-advocating-infanticide-worse-than-blackface/2768277002/
12 https://fredericksburg.com/opinion/columns/commentary-governors-cuomo-northam-do-not-represent-millennials/article_140b5cde-9603-5d25-b475-baae429ac780.html

It may sound hyperbolic but it's true: Barack Hussein Obama, Hillary Clinton, Joe Biden, and their friends are enemies of freedom. They hate low taxes, they hate business, and they hate guns. They want to take away your guns, your freedom, your freedom of speech, and your freedom of religion. I am an unabashed supporter of President Donald Trump, the greatest U.S. president we have ever had.

I also strongly believe that Reagan was one of our greatest presidents, helping lead the United States into a new era, an economic boon after four years of weak and stupid leadership by President Jimmy Carter. President Trump had to clean up the complete and utter mess left by the high-spending, high-taxation, protosocialist agenda of President Obama. Obama left countries burning and people without hope (ironically, he had campaigned on restoring hope), and he regularly divided Americans, inciting racial hatred for one another.

The Left has always found God verbiage offensive. From replacing "Merry Christmas" with "Happy Holidays" to seeking to erase "In God we trust" on our money, the movement has sought to erase all references to God.

Further, if our nation is under the authority of God and His watchful eye, as the thinking goes, it hinders our freedom. We can't be comfortable redefining liberty as "doing whatever we desire." We can't be comfortable killing four thousand innocent preborn children each day and redefining marriage, sex, and gender without feeling a touch of guilt. From the Democrats' perspective, God had to go.[13]

---

[13] https://www.churchmilitant.com/news/article/dems-agenda-strip-god-from-american-life

Obama started off dividing the country early in his presidency by trying to pit police officers against African Americans when he falsely, and without evidence, claimed that a police officer had acted "stupidly" when he asked a professor to identify himself while at his home. As he would regularly do, President Obama tried to stoke racial fears and divide Americans, and I'm going to give a few examples. It's important as you read this book to understand how Trump became an unlikely hero that united many Americans after Obama created a racial divide.

The Heritage Foundation's Hans von Spakovsky explained Obama's history of division really well in a 2017 article.[14] Here's an excerpt:

> Eight years of Obama's leadership has left America demonstrably weaker and more divided. Rather than the promised "healing"—racial and other—the Obama era frayed the ties that bind us.
>
> It began when his Justice Department dropped an open-and-shut voter intimidation case against the New Black Panther Party. It was essentially a declaration that his administration would use the Voting Rights Act to protect only certain races.
>
> There followed a steady stream of false claims that America was an inherently racist society with a biased judicial and law enforcement system. Obama rekindled a racial divide that had been steadily disappearing in American society.

---

[14] https://www.heritage.org/political-process/commentary/obamas-legacy-weaker-and-more-divided-america

In 2018, Senator Marco Rubio explained on Twitter how Obama divided the country:

> Pres. Obama is right. It is wrong for a President to use divisive language, such as:
> 1. Call all opponents of same-sex marriage bigots
> 2. Call the Pro-Life movement a "War on Women"
> 3. Call all immigration enforcement advocates racists
> 4. Call the GOP the enemy of Hispanics"[15]

Even the Associated Press had to admit that Obama largely failed to heal the country—in fact, that he heavily divided the country:

> And his presidency did not usher in racial harmony. Rather, both blacks and whites believe race relations have deteriorated, according to polls. Mounting tensions over police shootings of African-Americans prompted protests in several cities and the emergence of the Black Lives Matter movement.[16]

But people like Donald Trump and Ronald Reagan were champions of freedom. They supported gun rights, they supported freedom of speech and religion, and they supported your freedom to live your own life.

At a dinner for the National Rifle Association, President Reagan said:

---

15 https://twitter.com/marcorubio/status/1038390674884907008?ref_src
=twsrc%5Etfw%7Ctwcamp%5Etweetembed%7Ctwterm%5E10383906
74884907008%7Ctwgr%5E&ref_url=https%3A%2F%2Fwww.usatoday.
com%2Fstory%2Fnews%2Fpolitics%2Fonpolitics%2F2018%2F09%2F
10%2Fconservatives-attack-obama-speech%2F1254935002%2F

16 https://apnews.com/29b24a7985a442d8b890261da99cad86/
Obama-racial-legacy:-Pride,-promise,-regret-_-and-deep-rift

No group does more to promote gun safety and respect for the laws of this land than the NRA, and I thank you. Still, we've both heard the charge that supporting gun owners' rights encourages a violent, shoot-'em-up society. But just a minute. Don't they understand that most violent crimes are not committed by decent, law-abiding citizens? They're committed by career criminals. Guns don't make criminals. Hardcore criminals use guns. And locking them up, the hardcore criminals up, and throwing away the key is the best gun-control law we could ever have. When I was governor of California, we dealt with gun control—we added five to fifteen years to the sentence of any criminal who, while committing a crime, had a gun in his possession, whether he used that gun or not. Now, I'm even more convinced than ever that this is the right approach if they're going to talk about something to do with guns and crime.[17]

President Trump, also at an NRA dinner, said:

We believe in the rule of law. And we will always protect and defend the Constitution of the United States. And there are some people that are running right now, I don't think they have that number one on their list.

We believe that children should be taught to love our country, honor our history, and always respect our great American flag.

And we believe in the right to self-defense and the right to protect your family, your community, and your loved ones. We believe in the wisdom of our Founders.

---

[17] https://www.reaganfoundation.org/media/128658/nra.pdf

And we believe in freedom and liberty and the right to keep and bear arms.[18]

Reagan and Trump defended freedom, as shown in the above speeches to the NRA in support of gun rights. President Obama never would have attended an NRA meeting—unless he thought they were turning their guns in! Likewise for the weak and bumbling Joe Biden, who supports gun rights in speeches only when he thinks it helps solidify his fake blue-collar credentials.

Middle America—and this is something the enemies of freedom, like Kamala Harris and Nancy Pelosi, will never understand—supports gun rights. People like Harris and Pelosi have their high-paid security details, armed guards, and Capitol police, but you and I often have to defend ourselves. Harris, ironically, wants to be able to personally own guns but does not want other people to own guns.

In 2020, I released a book comparing Donald Trump, the greatest American president to ever live, with Winston Churchill, the greatest prime minister to ever lead the United Kingdom. The book was well-liked, and President Trump tweeted his support for it many times.

I am now writing this as the 2020 election heats up, in the midst of an economic crisis caused by the Wuhan virus, also known as Coronavirus or COVID-19. I still firmly believe that Trump is the greatest U.S. president we have ever had. He inspires hope in many Americans, and not just conservative Republicans. Small-business owners trust that he will cut

---

[18] https://www.whitehouse.gov/briefings-statements/remarks-president-trump-nra-ila-leadership-forum-indianapolis/

taxes for them and not squash them under the heavy hand of government. Christians appreciate how he fights for religious liberty and scientific truth on gender, and how he wants to end abortion.

In his 2020 State of the Union address, President Trump said:

> After decades of flat and falling incomes, wages are rising fast—and, wonderfully, they are rising fastest for low-income workers, who have seen a 16 percent pay increase since my election. This is a blue-collar boom..... Our roaring economy has, for the first time ever, given many former prisoners the ability to get a great job and a fresh start. This second chance at life is made possible because we passed landmark criminal justice reform into law. Everybody said that criminal justice reform couldn't be done, but I got it done, and the people in this room got it done.[19]

He inspires in the American people a confidence that has not been seen in decades—since, honestly, the presidency of Ronald Reagan, who inspired millions to believe in something better than the economic-malaise days of President Carter.

In his book *Trump: How to Get Rich*, Trump explains that a leader must be honest and decisive. He writes, "If you equivocate, it's an indication you're unsure of yourself and what you're doing. It's also what politicians do all the time, and I find it inappropriate, insulting, and condescending."

This is the guiding philosophy Trump carried with him into the White House. And as the president, he has made sure to

---

[19]   https://www.whitehouse.gov/briefings-statements/remarks-president-trump-state-union-address-3/

listen to many people, to speak the truth, and to be open about what he believes but also to be open to other ideas. He has demonstrated an innate ability to feel the pulse of America and has used that to help all Americans, no matter their religion, race, or gender.

When weak leaders like Obama are confronted with a problem—a nuclear-armed Iran, for example—their default decision is to run away or hand over the keys to the kingdom, so to speak, to the institutions and people they are afraid of, whether it's the Brookings Institution or Chris Cuomo on CNN. This is what Obama did when he let radical Islamic leaders write the terms of Iran's nuclear enrichment program, or when he let socialist French bureaucrats and Chinese business leaders work hand in hand to write the disastrous anti-freedom, anti-American Paris Accords, which President Trump was right to withdraw from. Obama once again allowed foreign governments to circumvent our American system of checks and balances, just as President Carter did.

In his 2015 campaign-kickoff speech, Trump said:

> Our country is in serious trouble. We don't have victories anymore. We used to have victories, but we don't have them. When was the last time anybody saw us beating, let's say, China in a trade deal? They kill us. I beat China all the time. All the time.
>
> When did we beat Japan at anything? They send their cars over by the millions, and what do we do? When was the last time you saw a Chevrolet in Tokyo? It doesn't exist, folks. They beat us all the time.
>
> When do we beat Mexico at the border? They're laughing at us, at our stupidity. And now they are beating

us economically. They are not our friend, believe me. But they're killing us economically.[20]

Blue-collar voters supported President Trump because they knew he would protect their right to bear arms, he would make sure that well-paying fracking and oil jobs would stay open and even expand, and he supported what they believed in and wouldn't denigrate them as "bitter clingers," as "Divider in Chief" Obama did. Trump has supported people who wake up every day and work for a living, unlike those high-paid bureaucrats who scheme all day on how to screw over average Americans. It's people like President Reagan and President Trump who have turned out to be unlikely heroes in their fight against the globalist elites.

As Trump said in 2019:

> Under the previous administration, our leaders rejected American energy and they rejected ethanol. They imposed radical restrictions on our farmers and ethanol producers. And they refused to even allow talk of E15 [a gasoline blended with ethanol] during the busiest driving months of the year. And as you know, we took it from eight months to twelve beautiful months. That's another big factor.... America must never again be held hostage to foreign suppliers of energy as we were under the Obama-Biden— Sleepy Joe—group. Sleepy Joe.[21]

---

20   https://time.com/3923128/donald-trump-announcement-speech/
21   https://www.whitehouse.gov/briefings-statements/
      remarks-president-trump-renewable-energy/

Finally, the disaffected middle liked him because he would shake up NATO, appoint solid judges, and break through political correctness and cancel culture. As he said in 2018:

> Prior to last year, where I attended my first meeting, it was going down—the amount of money being spent by countries was going down and down very substantially. And now, it's going up very substantially. And commitments were made. Only five of twenty-nine countries were making their commitment. And that's now changed. The commitment was at 2 percent. Ultimately, that'll be going up quite a bit higher than that.[22]

And again showing his brilliance, Trump added:

> I told people that I'd be very unhappy if they didn't up their commitments very substantially, because the United States has been paying a tremendous amount, probably 90 percent of the cost of NATO. And now, people are going to start and countries are going to start upping their commitments. So I let them know yesterday, actually. I was surprised that you didn't pick it up; it took until today. But yesterday, I let them know that I was extremely unhappy with what was happening, and they have substantially upped their commitment, yeah. And now we're very happy and have a very, very powerful, very, very strong NATO, much stronger than it was two days ago.[23]

---

22   https://www.whitehouse.gov/briefings-statements/remarks-president-trump-press-conference-nato-summit-brussels-belgium/

23   https://www.whitehouse.gov/briefings-statements/remarks-president-trump-press-conference-nato-summit-brussels-belgium/

A leftist professor at the University of Pennsylvania, Amy Castro Baker, conceded the reasons Trump won the election in 2016, in an interview shortly after the election. She stated:

> We're talking a lot about the middle class. We're talking a lot about the working class. That's important. That's crucial. It's clearly played a role in the election.... Pay has stagnated, while at the same time the cost of living is going up. We talk a lot about wage gaps and pay gaps, but it's really more about a wealth gap. We're talking about communities of people, both in those rural areas that came out strong for Trump and also in the city, where historically folks have voted for the Democratic Party. What we're seeing are a real erosion of assets and wealth. People just don't have things to protect them in the economy anymore.[24]

Curiously, similar arguments were made in support of Reagan, who defeated the weak and ineffective President Jimmy Carter in 1980. Much like Joe Biden today, Carter portrayed himself as a down-to-earth Christian guy who was in touch with the common man. But then he became president, and millions of people lost their jobs and energy prices skyrocketed.

Henry Olsen, a fellow at the Ethics and Public Policy Center, wrote after the 2016 election that Trump's election was a sign that Reagan's influence was returning to the Republican Party. He stated that the Reagan presidency displayed blue-collar conservatism in many ways, but principally in tax cuts:

> During the Reagan presidency, first it manifested itself that he was cutting taxes for everybody. He cut tax rates for

---

[24] https://knowledge.wharton.upenn.edu/article/why-middle-america-voted-for-trump/

everybody. He indexed the brackets for inflation. When he did his tax reform, he also increased the personal exemptions so that millions of people were removed from the tax rolls entirely.

All families—all individuals—got a tax break even if their rates didn't come down very much.

So you had both a president who is trying to create jobs and increase private sector opportunity, who is giving tax cuts to everybody, not just the top 1 percent, and protecting people at or below the median income from cuts in their benefits.[25]

There are many other similarities between President Reagan and President Trump, which we will explore throughout this book. However, the two were not ideological twins. Whereas Reagan was softer-spoken, Trump is, in a good way, brash and can be loud. Whereas Reagan often supported dovish policies on trade and towards China, Trump has taken a more hardline approach on China and trade. However, like Churchill benefitted from his predecessors, Trump has benefitted from progress made by Reagan. At the same time, both Reagan and Trump protected gun rights, supported ending abortion (pro-life policies), and saw the role of America as leader but not as policeman. In fact, one of the biggest surprises, in a very good way, is how President Trump has kept the United States out of endless wars and has tried hard to end our engagement in places like Afghanistan. In 1984, Reagan spoke on the topic of involvement in war:

---

[25]   https://www.aei.org/economics/reaganism-for-the-working-class-a-short-read-qa-with-henry-olsen/

History teaches that wars begin when governments believe the price of aggression is cheap. To keep the peace, we and our allies must be strong enough to convince any potential aggressor that war could bring no benefit, only disaster. So, when we neglected our defenses, the risks of serious confrontation grew.

Three years ago, we embraced a mandate from the American people to change course. And we have. With the support of the American people and the Congress, we halted America's decline. Our economy is now in the midst of the best recovery since the sixties. Our defenses are being rebuilt, our alliances are solid, and our commitment to defend our values has never been more clear.

America's recovery may have taken Soviet leaders by surprise. They may have counted on us to keep weakening ourselves. They've been saying for years that our demise was inevitable. They said it so often, they probably started believing it. Well, if so, I think they can see now they were wrong.[26]

President Reagan did try to keep us out of overseas foreign conflicts, preferring instead to build up our military and use diplomacy to protect American interests.

As U.S. senator Rand Paul explained in a 2013 speech:

Reagan's foreign policy was robust but also restrained. He pulled no punches in telling Mr. Gorbachev to "tear down that wall." He did not shy away from labeling the Soviet Union as an evil empire. But he also sat down with Gorbachev and negotiated meaningful reductions in

---

[26] https://www.nytimes.com/1984/01/17/world/transcript-of-reagan-s-speech-on-soviet-american-relations.html

nuclear weapons.... [T]he truth is that Reagan used clear messages of communism's evil and clear exposition of America's strength to contain and ultimately to transcend the Soviet Union.[27]

Paul made similar comments, which we will touch on later, that got him in trouble with the mainstream media and the foreign policy establishment; all because he spoke in favor of peaceful talks that Trump held with Vladimir Putin.

Throughout this book, I have relied on a variety of sources to get a full picture of both Reagan and Trump. Of course, I am a Republican and a conservative. I have been outspoken in my support of Trump. Regardless, I have relied on original source material, contemporary and historical analysis, and verifiable data as much as possible. But of course, I do support Trump and believe Reagan was a great president as well, and I would have voted for him if I'd had to opportunity to do so.

Unlike the mainstream media, I am open in my political beliefs and admit I am not an objective, disinterested historian (if such a person even exists). I've provided a list of the sources I have drawn on, and you're certainly welcome to review these sources and come to your own conclusion. This books relies on more than one hundred sources, as well as pages and pages of speeches by Trump and Reagan, and you can draw on these sources to make your own judgments.

As another note, I do not spend much time in this book covering the historical life of Reagan or Trump. There are plenty of great books about their early lives and their early careers. This

---

[27] https://www.politico.com/story/2013/02/rand-paul-likens-policies-to-ronald-reagans-087258

book is about how Trump and Reagan were unlikely heroes and how they led a nation. As I write this book, the 2020 election is several months away. Hopefully, there will be a second term for President Trump. Regardless, the four years he has been in office so far give us a good place to start with his legacy.

This book is being written leading up to the 2020 election during a manufactured coronavirus crisis. Former vice president Joe Biden is running for president despite a lengthy record of lying, racism, and sexual harassment. Of course the mainstream media, the deep state, and the Swamp want to see Biden win in the same way that they wanted to see Hillary Clinton win, so that they can continue to machinate and pull the levers of power to hurt the average American.

Thankfully, Americans benefitted from the leadership of Reagan and Trump, a topic that we will explore in depth in this book. Both presidents learned those leadership skills through a variety of roles that are surprisingly unusual for conservative Republicans. For example, Reagan and Trump both came from Hollywood—Reagan as a former actor and acting union president, and Trump figuratively coming from Hollywood, where he was wildly successful with *The Apprentice* after an already stellar career as the best real estate developer in the city of New York, if not the United States of America.

Reagan served as governor of California, something he did well save for his mistakes on issues like abortion, which we will touch on later. He did a much better job, of course, than the terrible leader Governor Gavin Newsom has done. Newsom is one of the country's worst governors and has completely botched his state's response to coronavirus. He has also been an embarrassment to the state of California, failing to lead the state and instead wasting time on trying to stop Trump from being the enormously successful president he has been.

In a speech on government waste in 1981, President Reagan said:

> I also want every member of this administration—from those in the Cabinet, to the sub-Cabinet, to Federal employees beginning their careers today—to understand that we will not tolerate fraud, waste, and abuse of the taxpayers' dollars. Every allegation of wrongdoing, every investigative lead will be pursued thoroughly and objectively. The vital element in any program designed to fight fraud and waste is the willingness of employees to come forward when they see this sort of activity. They must be assured that when they "blow the whistle," they will be protected and their information properly investigated. During the past few decades, government programs have multiplied and expenditures have grown by quantum leaps. But during this time, little attention has been paid to the serious problems of mismanagement and criminal fraud. One Department of Justice study has revealed that in social programs, fraud alone could be as much as 1 to 10 percent of the expenditures for those programs.
>
> It is time to put a halt to this waste and wrongdoing. These steps I have mentioned today represent only a beginning in one of the toughest and most important programs this administration will undertake: eliminating waste and fraud, and restoring the public's faith in the integrity of government.[28]

---

[28] https://www.reaganlibrary.gov/research/speeches/41681a

Reagan was a much better leader of California than Newsom has been. In 1969, he swiftly shut down violent protests in Berkeley—actually riots—for example. He pioneered new ways of government and worked to shrink the size of government, going at both Republicans and Democrats. As an actor, he wasn't coming from a field of high-paid consultancy. He learned from his experience as a governor, an actor, and a broadcaster how to articulate a good message and how to hear back from the average American. As early as 1966, in the announcement of his candidacy for governor of California, Reagan said of the antiwar protests in Berkeley:

> [D]o we no longer think it necessary to teach self-respect, self-discipline, and respect for law and order? Will we allow a great university to be brought to its knees by a noisy dissident minority? Will we meet their neurotic vulgarities with vacillation and weakness? Or will we tell those entrusted with administering the university we expect them to enforce a code based on decency, common sense, and dedication to the high and noble purpose of that university?[29]

As the website The Federalist noted of the Berkeley situation:

> Not unlike another wildly popular, yet wildly unpopular politician, Reagan was elected partly to restore law and order. A group of protestors put the governor to the test in 1969. They had been using a vacant plot of land for protests against the Vietnam War and decided to block

---

[29]   https://www.americanrhetoric.com/speeches/ronaldreagancalgovcandidacy.htm

the university from developing it. The day in May 1969 when the university attempted to erect a fence around the plot of land is called "Bloody Thursday." A rally called to protest the action drew thousands and soon turned into a riot. Reagan ordered the Berkeley police and California Highway Patrol to shut it down.... Someone in the crowd shouts that Reagan should have negotiated with the students. Reagan, with the incredulity of someone who understands that youth don't run the world for a reason, says: "Negotiate? What is to negotiate? All of it began the first time some of you who know better and are old enough to know better let young people think that they have the right to choose the laws they would obey as long as they were doing it in the name of social protest."[30]

Trump has stood up for free enterprise and American business while also standing up against cronyism and corporate welfare and protecting American ingenuity. We will explore throughout this book how Trump and Reagan displayed incredible leadership, foresight, and support for red-blooded Americans throughout their presidencies. Neither man was predictably presidential material, let alone a *conservative* president. But both men rose to the occasion.

During his 1966 speech announcing his candidacy for the governor position in California, Reagan described a situation very similar to what he would face sixteen years later when he defeated Carter, one of the worst presidents in modern history:

---

[30] https://thefederalist.com/2017/04/24/heres-ronald-reagan-college-kids-went-ape-uc-berkeley/

Some of those problems have grown faster than the population, and in that we're number one in the nation. Now all of us are concerned that in our growth we don't destroy the very things that brought us here in the first place. It won't matter if the sky is big and bluer out here if you can't see it for smog. And all our elbow room and open space won't mean much if the unsolved problems are higher than the hills.

Cracks have appeared in our economy. The unemployment rate is almost 40 percent higher than the rest of the nation. And we lead the nation in bankruptcies and business failures. We've dropped from sixth to thirteenth among the states with regard to new industries locating here. There's no way to count the jobs that don't exist, because they didn't come here. But we can count very easily the eight hundred jobs that disappeared in Palo Alto when an aircraft plant moved to the East Coast.

He added:

But their approach to the solution of our problems reveals a basic disagreement in philosophy. They're dedicated to a belief in rule by administrative edict, with more and more control and regulation of the economy, and of our lives. Just recently, a report of the Commission on California State Government Organization and [Economy] admitted there's no way to count the boards, commissions, and bureaus in the executive branch. A legislative analyst made a partial count and listed 276—fifty-three appointed in the last few years.

Now, we're told that every increase in government is caused by increase in population. But government is increased four times as fast as population; and total state expenditures are up ten times as much. Budget deficits aren't met by sound fiscal changes, but by one-time wind-falls, sweeping the problem under the rug with gimmicks: advancing the collection of corporate income tax one year, sales tax the next.[31]

President Trump, in just a few years, has restored respect for America and the American system of law and order and free enterprise. He has accomplished this despite having to overcome the tremendous damage wrought on America by President Obama. He won over support from America's front-line public safety personnel, such as our military and police officers. Consider what Trump said in 2020 about our brave law enforcement officers. For context, this speech came during a wave of leftist violence from the Black Lives Matter and Antifa movements in cities like Portland, Oregon.

In recent weeks, law enforcement has become the target of a dangerous assault by the radical left. The left-wing extremists have spread mayhem throughout the streets of different cities—in particular, Portland. If you look, Portland is one. Seattle, really, would be another. We had hundreds of millions of dollars' worth of equipment— really good military equipment, good stuff. And a lot of it was protective. It was defensive equipment, where—like, vehicles that are very strong in terms of defense capability, where you wouldn't get hurt; where the windows are, you know, shatterproof, etc., and bulletproof.

---

[31] https://www.americanrhetoric.com/speeches/ronaldreagancalgovcan-didacy.htm

And we gave that out to our police departments. It was sitting there gaining dust. That was the only thing it was gaining, was dust. And we gave that out to all of our police departments all over the country. And you have no idea: every place—every time I go someplace, the police thank me for that.[32]

And this is, of course, just one way that Trump won over the police. They responded with support, as he won over numerous endorsements from our brave law enforcement officers.[33][34] The Florida police union head said:

I spelled it out on what's going on not just in Florida but across this country that, "Hey, you know what, we're getting beat up. We're getting used like a punching bag and we're tired of it and President Donald Trump has been there for us. He supported us.

Said a Michigan police union leader as the Democratic Party and far-left activists sought to defund the police:

He supports the police, while the previous administration preferred to insult them or to find them guilty without due process. Our officers are under attack and are being told to "stand down." At a time when civic leaders are choosing to tolerate televised felonies because a group of people is "offended," we need real leadership."[35]

---

[32] https://www.whitehouse.gov/briefings-statements/remarks-president-trump-meeting-national-association-police-organizations-leadership/

[33] https://www.foxnews.com/politics/nyc-police-union-endorses-trump-for-the-2020-presidency

[34] https://www.foxnews.com/media/florida-police-union-backs-trump

[35] https://www.mlive.com/public-interest/2020/07/michigans-largest-police-group-sticks-with-trump-citing-opposition-to-law-enforcement-reform.html

One thing that Trump did that directly relates to his ability to win over people and become an unlikely hero is how he won over his adversaries in his own party very quickly. It's not necessary to go into the bitterness of the 2016 Republican National Committee primaries in depth, but suffice it to say that many in that party vehemently, and wrongly, opposed Trump. But many of those people made the right decision to reevaluate and ended up coming out in support of him.

Consider:

▶ Senator Rand Paul thanked President Trump for his peaceful approach to international relations. When Trump met with Vladimir Putin in 2018, Paul went on CNN and said, "The big picture is that we should be engaged with Russia. It would be a mistake not to have open lines of communication with them."[36]

▶ Also in 2018, Senator Ted Cruz, a 2016 rival of President Trump's, praised him in a *Time* magazine special:

> President Trump is a flash-bang grenade thrown into Washington by the forgotten men and women of America. The fact that his first year as Commander in Chief disoriented and distressed members of the media and political establishment is not a bug but a feature.
>
> The same cultural safe spaces that blinkered coastal elites to candidate Trump's popularity have rendered them blind to President Trump's achievements on behalf of ordinary Americans. While pundits obsessed over tweets, he worked with

---

[36] https://www.courier-journal.com/story/news/politics/2020/01/31/kentucky-sen-rand-paul-has-gone-trump-critic-devout-ally/4610465002/

Congress to cut taxes for struggling families. While wealthy celebrities announced that they would flee the country, he fought to bring back jobs and industries to our shores. While talking heads predicted Armageddon, President Trump's strong stand against North Korea put Kim Jong Un back on his heels.

President Trump is doing what he was elected to do: disrupt the status quo. That scares the heck out of those who have controlled

Washington for decades, but for millions of Americans, their confusion is great fun to watch."[37]

▶ Radio host Glenn Beck, an early critic of Trump and a supporter of candidate Ted Cruz, explained why he would likely be voting for Trump in 2020:[38]

I think so. Yeah, I think so. He especially now with the left is gone insane [sic]. Donald Trump had no record when he was running and anything that he had ever said is pretty liberal. And he's a new Yorker and I, you know, I know New Yorkers and their conservative is, you know, a Texas Marxist. And I just didn't think he would do any of the things he said. I was for Ted Cruz. I didn't think Ted Cruz would have done half of what Donald Trump has done with Israel.[39]

▶ Finally, consider the praise from former Wisconsin governor Scott Walker. In 2020, he correctly and proudly

---

[37] https://time.com/collection/most-influential-people-2018/5217621/donald-trump-2/

[38] https://www.realclearpolitics.com/video/2020/02/24/sharyl_attkisson_interviews_glenn_beck_i_think_ill_vote_for_trump_especially_now_with_the_left_is_gone_insane.html

[39] https://www.realclearpolitics.com/video/2020/02/24/sharyl_attkisson_interviews_glenn_beck_i_think_ill_vote_for_trump_especially_now_with_the_left_is_gone_insane.html

praised Trump for condemning violence against people of faith and standing in front of St. John's church across from the White House.

President Reagan likewise drew praise from many of his critics, including his 1980 rival George H. W. Bush, who would end up serving eight years as Reagan's vice president and then another four years as president, something most political experts agree was essentially Reagan's "third term."

Many of the malcontents in the Republican Party, those who tried to undermine Reagan, ended up praising him and realizing their mistakes.

Reagan and Trump turned out to be unlikely heroes. They fought to drain the Swamp. They fought off the deep state, they bucked their party, and they fought for the American people.

Reagan and Trump were the American heroes we needed. As a legal immigrant to the United States, I can only hope that I can help America even one-tenth the amount that our great presidents Trump and Reagan did.

CHAPTER 1

ORIGINS

"The deep-state Republicans are alive and well and doing what you'd expect them to be doing. They are living proof that President Donald Trump is a genuine change agent. The world he is changing is their world, and they hate him for it."

—Newt Gingrich, former
speaker of the House[40]

"Trump is the one guy doing it. And they don't like it. They don't know how to put up with it, but they know that they hate Trump and they want to get rid of him. And [Richard] Grenell is pointing out, like Colin Powell, all these others, Mitt Romney running around joining the Biden campaign when they would never, ever, do that except for their hatred of Trump, it's because Trump is still pushing back and trying to drain the Swamp, meaning he's still succeeding."

—Rush Limbaugh[41]

40 https://www.foxnews.com/opinion/anti-trump-republicans-rather-sup-port-biden-pelosi-and-schumer-newt-gingrich

41 https://www.rushlimbaugh.com/daily/2020/06/15/ric-grenell-trump-is-breaking-the-swamp-system/

"We're here to cut back on waste and mismanagement; to eliminate unnecessary, restrictive regulations that make it harder for the American economy to compete and harder for American workers to find jobs; to drain the Swamp of overtaxation, overregulation, and runaway inflation that has dangerously eroded our free way of life."

—President Ronald Reagan[42]

"We hear much of special interest groups. Well, our concern must be for a special interest group that has been too long neglected. It knows no sectional boundaries or ethnic and racial divisions, and it crosses political party lines. It is made up of men and women who raise our food, patrol our streets, man our mines and factories, teach our children, keep our homes, and heal us when we're sick—professionals, industrialists, shopkeepers, clerks, cabbies, and truckdrivers. They are, in short, 'We the people,' this breed called Americans."

—President Ronald Reagan[43]

President Donald Trump and President Ronald Reagan were unlikely heroes to America and drainers of the Swamp. They came out in support of Middle America and of the forgotten man. They did this in the face of relentless lies and attacks from the fake news media, the well-funded globalist network, and the big business and George Soros–related groups that wanted to undermine faith in American democracy, free enterprise, and the Constitution.

---

[42] https://www.reaganlibrary.gov/12082b

[43] https://www.reaganlibrary.gov/research/speeches/inaugural-address-january-20-1981

Both men, as mentioned, did not start out as policy wonks. They did not intern on Capitol Hill, work as campaign managers, or start off as state reps or mayors as part of a grand plan to one day run for president. Neither showed up on any globalist plan to install him as president or made any backroom list among the party's kingmakers.

In April 2017, just a few months into the Trump administration, conservative radio host Dennis Prager explained well how Trump was an unlikely conservative hero:

> What I do know is that they ought to be deeply appreciative of him, and deeply grateful to luck or Providence, and certainly to Trump himself, that he was elected president. First, it is unlikely that any other Republican would have defeated Hillary Clinton. Second, he has not only surpassed many of our expectations, he has thus far governed in a manner more consistent with conservative principles than any president since Ronald Reagan, and arguably since Calvin Coolidge.[44]

Prager acknowledged that he had initially opposed Trump, but said he had quickly come around to supporting him as the president. He explained why we should support Trump and view him as a great president:

> He has repealed many of the Obama energy regulations that would strangle the American economy. He doesn't believe that carbon-induced warming of the planet will destroy the human race, the greatest of the innumerable hysterias the left manufactures and then believes in.

---

[44] https://www.nationalreview.com/2017/04/donald-trump-conservative-hero/

He has appointed as secretary of education a woman who, as a billionaire, could easily have devoted her life to enjoying her wealth, but instead has fought for American students and their parents to be able to choose their schools just as the wealthy do. And the president has taken on the teachers' unions, the only group that has ever given American teachers a bad name.

He has appointed a woman to be ambassador to the United Nations who is calling the UN the naked emperor that it is. And now America is backing, rather than subverting, Israel in that benighted institution.

And now he has vowed, after decades of American obsequiousness, to confront the sociopathic North Korean regime.

The American media—most particularly its elite—no longer even feign objective reporting. It is solely an arm of the left and of the Democratic party; its task being the delegitimization of the Trump presidency.

I borrow from my recent book, *Trump and Churchill: Defenders of Western Civilization*, to explain how Trump and Reagan helped protect Western civilization:

A respect for religious freedom, including the rights of people to worship in the religion they choose or to not worship in a religion at all. It means that the government and society at large respect the rights of Catholics, Muslims, Jews, Hindus, Buddhists, Evangelicals, and so forth to pray publicly, to open schools that teach religious values, to run for office or be appointed a judge, or to share their faith in any other voluntary, nonforceful way they choose....

A right to the freedom of speech, including the right to criticize or praise one's government; to write books, pamphlets, or on social media about one's views on any issue, including the right to speak out against the government without fear of reprisal. It's worth noting here that despite the fake news media's screeching against Trump, he actually is known to be one of the most talkative and open presidents of recent times, and even among all politicians, going back to his old days as a businessman in Queens, New York....

Support for free enterprise, including a system of limited taxation, property rights, the right to open a business, the right to be free from government corruption and coercion, and a promise that the government will not punish someone for marrying your business practices with your religious and philosophical views (for example, not punishing Christian bakers for not making cakes for homosexual weddings)....

By its nature, a Western civilization–based government and people must also speak out and oppose systems that would strip away these rights, such as racist, eugenicist fascism; anti-religious communism; and the hateful ideology of all other totalitarian ideologies, including fascism, communism, and a caliphate. All of these hateful ideologies are a form of collectivism, which is the ideology most opposed to Western civilization, because it seeks to impose on all people a top-down approach that decides who has value and who does not. Communists say capitalists do not have value; fascists say Jews do not have value; caliphates say that non-Muslims do not have value. All of these systems inherently violate the ideals of Western civilization.

Thankfully, they were both victorious, because if they had not been, horrible situations would have ensued.

We now turn to what Trump and Reagan had to overcome to become unlikely heroes and Swamp drainers.

The script was set for 2016. Jeb Bush, the son of one president and the brother of another, had raised hundreds of millions of dollars to take on presumptive Democratic presidential nominee Hillary Clinton. He had lined up endorsements from his father's and brother's friends, former and current D.C. Swamp monsters who regularly took advantage of the revolving door, moving between government and big business, and lobbying as if the door were always open and never stuck. Those who were part of the big money Establishment of the Republican Party were ready for Jeb Bush, knowing they could get fat off lucrative crony trade deals and the financing of more endless overseas wars. They knew that in Jeb Bush, they'd have their man.

And after all, though Jeb Bush had a record of being pro-life and supporting gun rights, they felt sure that he wouldn't make such divisive issues central to his campaign. He'd talk about economic policies and bringing people together. And of course, he would keep, and probably open up further, the illegal immigration spigot to allow more and more illegal immigrants to come in and undercut American workers. The big banks and the big money fundraisers for Jeb Bush wanted to ensure cheap credit and cheap labor so they could prop up their own investments, the working man be damned. They don't like people like you and me; they want to tear us down to pad their own bank accounts.

On the Democratic side, Hillary Clinton was ready. She had served as a senator from New York, a state she never lived in until later in her husband's presidency. Then, for some reason, President Obama appointed her secretary of state. While this decision was likely made to keep Clinton's image elevated for a presidential election in 2016, it likely ended up hurting her, as it once again exposed her lack of judgment and poor leadership skills. Obama should have appointed her to a less controversial and less judgment-based position, like secretary for the Department of Transportation or Department of the Treasury (her banking friends would have liked that!).

She too would be a handmaiden to Wall Street and globalist interests. After all, it was she who bragged to the wealthy elite that she would open up a free flow of illegal immigration, trade, and money to enrich their bank accounts. It was Clinton, after all, who told bankers in 2013, "My dream is a hemispheric common market, with open trade and open borders, sometime in the future with energy that is as green and sustainable as we can get it, powering growth and opportunity for every person in the Hemisphere."[45] She was another favored candidate of Wall Street. After all, they poured tens of millions of dollars into her campaign, because they knew she would serve *their* interests, not the interests of the American people.[46]

And this leads us again to how the Establishment, how the D.C. Swamp monsters, did not want Trump to be president. And they did not want Reagan to be president either. In this book, as mentioned, we will explore the ways that Trump and Reagan took on the Swamp and became unlikely heroes to millions of

---

[45]   https://www.washingtontimes.com/news/2016/oct/8/hillary-clinton-dreams-open-borders-leaked-speech-/

[46]   https://www.cnbc.com/2016/05/26/wall-street-gives-hillary-clinton-27m-but-love-affair-may-not-last.html

conservatives, libertarians, and Middle Americans. We will talk about how they pursued an aggressive economic agenda to free the American economy and put more money in the pockets of the American worker. We will talk about how they refused to let the globalist foreign policy elite write our policies, and instead put America first.

A Hollywood actor and union president. A New York real estate developer and socialite. High-paid political consultants and overpriced media relations experts would say that neither man could become president. Better to have an experienced patrician governor, or a senator who was part of numerous make-work committees and commissions (the more ribbons you cut, the better a president you will be, the Rick Wilsons and other political charlatans and bloodsuckers would say).

Or perhaps a "senior statesmen" who was well-respected for his bipartisanship. These are the people we need leading us, the thinking goes. After all, they can then staff government with their friends from the numerous lobbyist firms, media networks, and think tanks that abound between New York and Washington, D.C. They know all the "experts," after all. People who had full careers before becoming president, careers outside of federal government and outside of the Swamp, could never and should never become president, the permanent political class would argue. That's why they love Mitt Romney now—he says mean things about President Trump! And he's a nice guy!

Wait, I have a better idea! Let's have someone who started off out of college working in Congress, then ran for office, then failed to push through conservative policies, and then have him run on a presidential ticket! Or perhaps we could have a senator who has never faced a tough reelection on the ticket, someone who is always ready to "buck" his party when it means going against free-market, conservative principles but is never ready to do so when the party proposes more and more government spending and threats to our personal liberty.

That's who the Swamp wants. That's who the Establishment wants. That's why they were so excited about 2016 before Trump dominated in the primaries. They wanted Jeb Bush! With Bush and Hillary Clinton running against each other, the big banks, the military-industrial complex, the warmongers, and so on would win either way—they'd have a friendly Wall Street candidate who would invade countries left and right and enrich their bank accounts. You can imagine how giddy they were at the prospect of Clinton versus Bush—after all, they'd be guaranteed more endless wars, endless debt (which they could profit from), and big business–friendly policies. And likely there would not be as many high-profile battles over issues like guns, abortion, and marriage.

But then something interesting happened in 2016: the Establishment lost, just as it did in 1980. This is something few in the mainstream media predicted.

But both Reagan and Trump *did become president*. Both not only held the office but innovated within the office: Reagan left an indelible mark on the White House, and President Trump is leaving his mark. They faced down similar opponents, including D.C. Swamp monsters, the Establishment media, and even their own party. These groups regularly collude to try to bring down innovators, freedom lovers, and anyone who would dare release a bull at the six p.m. Georgetown receptions where the leaders of our country gather over cocktails to plot the demise of the average American citizen and patriot.

The real patriots, the ones who run stores, fight wars, and go to work every day to produce *value*, are the ones that the Establishment despises; these are the people Reagan represented and the legacy that President Trump represents now.

Both Reagan and Trump took on the Swamp monsters and have the scars to show for it. But importantly, Middle America, the people who keep America running, supported them for what they did.

Let's set the scene briefly for what I mean when I talk about the Establishment and draining the Swamp.

Adam Andrzejewski, founder of the government watchdog group Open the Books, has written numerous reports about the Swamp. In one report, called "Operation Drain the Swamp," he wrote:

> In America today, "the swamp" is a real thing: a permanent government within our government that will outlast this administration and the next one and the one after that. It has a massive architecture that can be measured. It is composed of tens of thousands of individuals and lobbyists—many of whom operate well outside the confines of Washington, D.C.

He noted:

> In the swamp, six-figure salaries are the norm; there are seventy-eight agencies where the average salary is one hundred thousand dollars or more;
>
> Federal bureaucrats are paid $1.1 million every minute, $65.6 million every hour, and over half a billion dollars per day;

In 2016, there were more than 330,000 disclosed federal bonuses paid;

There are more than thirty-five thousand lawyers in the administrative state. The army of lawyers in the employ of the federal government assures that no aspect of American life is untouched by the swamp's appendages;

The VA [Veterans Affairs] is offering anything but care for our great vets. While veterans were suffering at the hands of a broken bureaucratic machine, the VA doled out tens of thousands of undeserved performance bonuses: $150 million per year;

From 2015 to 2016 the VA made 20,711 new hires, but just 2,091 were doctors, continuing the historical 10:1 doctor to nondoctor employee hiring ratio;

In 2016, the VA employed 3,498 police officers at a total cost of $172 million—all names and locations of these officers, however, were redacted;

The average physician at the VA makes around $205,000 a year, meaning the VA could employ 840 doctors instead of 3,498 police officers."[47]

It's not just government watchdogs that recognize the problem of the Swamp. It's also the people who have worked within government and have seen the problems up close.

Richard Grenell, who served as U.S. ambassador to Germany and as acting director of national intelligence, praised Trump for "breaking the Swamp."

On Rush Limbaugh's show in June 2020, he said:

We have a real problem in Washington, D.C., because it's a system that is no longer really Republicans and Democrats

---

[47] https://www.openthebooks.com/operation_drain_the_swamp/

pushing against each other to create a good policy. It's no longer a fight between Republicans and Democrats. It's a fight between Washington and the rest of America. It's musical chairs from one agency to another. There's no outside thought. There's no outside perspective when someone like Donald Trump comes in and says, "Why are we doing it this way?" They attack him because he's breaking the system. He doesn't play by their rules.[48]

Grenell, who is gay, came under fire from the hardcore left and the homosexual community because he dared to work for Trump to advance his agenda to make America great again. Leftists like minorities only when they think *exactly like them*.

In reading this book and following the president, it's important to remember that the media do not like people like you and me. Even if you're just reading this but don't necessarily agree with me, they do not like you because you're at least open to hearing what I have to say. If you also happen to be Christian, pro-gun, and an Israel supporter, or you hold *any* conservative views, the media despise you. They don't want you to *think* for yourself! The biggest enemy, the biggest threat to the CNN and Beltway elite crowd is free thinkers.

The Swamp is a disgusting, ever-evolving monster that tries to eat up reformers like Trump and Reagan. It works every day to screw over average Americans to benefit the ruling class. The Swamp enriches itself at the trough of the taxpayer.

In April 2020, as the "fifteen days to slow the spread" of Coronavirus continued on and on and on, conservative

---

[48]   https://www.rushlimbaugh.com/daily/2020/06/15/ric-grenell-trump-is-breaking-the-swamp-system/

commentator Wayne Allyn Root wrote on the problem of the Swamp and trusting the elites. Addressing President Trump, he said:

> My audience loves and supports you. We have your back! Do you know who doesn't have your back? The Ivy League eggheads; the Washington, D.C., Swamp-dwelling politicians and bureaucrats; and the deep-state doctors surrounding you. No one elected Dr. Anthony Fauci president. No one elected Dr. Deborah Birx, Surgeon General Jerome Adams, or hapless Federal Reserve chair Jerome Powell, either. And for good reason. They care only about being loved by the media, using big government to solve every problem and never saying something for which they might be blamed.
>
> They're not my president.... You are!
>
> The academics and deep staters just pass the buck. They have scared Americans to death with worthless, flawed, worst-case computer models that never work in the real world."[49]

The Swamp gobbles up your hard-earned dollars and gives them to leftist organizations that advocate for policies with which you likely do not agree.

The Swamp pushes so-called diversity training and tolerance and inclusion education to government bureaucrats (that's probably why the government moves so slowly in providing actual services to constituents—that is, you and me).

---

[49] https://www.creators.com/read/wayne-allyn-root/04/20/mr-president-stop-listening-to-the-dc-swamp-politicians-deep-state-bureaucrats-and-ivy-league-eggheads

Angelo Codevilla, an adviser to President Reagan, has expounded on what the Swamp is in his many writings on what he calls the ruling class.

He has said that the battle is not Republicans versus Democrats; it's the ruling class versus the country party—that is, the party of people who represent most Americans. In 2010 he wrote:

> Who are these rulers, and by what right do they rule? How did America change from a place where people could expect to live without bowing to privileged classes to one in which, at best, they might have the chance to climb into them? What sets our ruling class apart from the rest of us?

The most widespread answers—by such as the *Times*'s Thomas Friedman and David Brooks—are schlock sociology. Supposedly, modern society became so complex and productive, the technical skills to run it so rare, that it called forth a new class of highly educated officials and cooperators in an ever less private sector. Similarly fanciful is Edward Goldberg's notion that America is now ruled by a "newocracy": a "new aristocracy who are the true beneficiaries of globalization—including the multinational manager, the technologist and the aspirational members of the meritocracy." In fact, our ruling class grew and set itself apart from the rest of us by its connection with ever bigger government, and above all by a certain attitude.

Other explanations are counterintuitive. Wealth? The heads of the class do live in our big cities' priciest enclaves and suburbs, from Montgomery County, Maryland, to Palo Alto, California, to Boston's Beacon Hill as well as in opulent university towns from Princeton to Boulder. But they are no wealthier than many Texas oilmen or California farmers, or than neighbors with whom they do not associate—just as the social science and humanities class that rules universities seldom associates with physicians and physicists. Rather, regardless of where they live, their social-intellectual circle includes people in the lucrative "nonprofit" and "philanthropic" sectors and public policy. What really distinguishes these privileged people demographically is that, whether in government power directly or as officers in companies, their careers and fortunes depend on government. They vote Democrat more consistently than those who live on any of America's Dr. Martin Luther King Jr. Streets. These socio-economic opposites draw their money and orientation from the same sources as the millions of teachers, consultants, and government employees in the middle ranks who aspire to be the former and identify morally with what they suppose to be the latter's grievances.[50]

They live in the poshest suburbs and get a kick out of the power they hold. That's the Swamp. That's the ruling class.

It's why Trump said so eloquently in his inaugural address the following:

> For too long, a small group in our nation's capital has reaped the rewards of government while the people have borne the cost.
>
> Washington flourished—but the people did not share in its wealth.
>
> Politicians prospered—but the jobs left, and the factories closed.

---

[50]   https://www.independent.org/publications/article.asp?id=4725

The Establishment protected itself, but not the citizens of our country.

Their victories have not been your victories; their triumphs have not been your triumphs; and while they celebrated in our nation's capital, there was little to celebrate for struggling families all across our land.

That all changes—starting right here, and right now, because this moment is your moment: it belongs to you.[51]

The Swamp also includes people like Kevin Clinesmith, an FBI attorney—meaning someone we U.S. taxpayers give money to, to protect us from crimes—who pled guilty to charges that he falsified information to carry out warrants as part of the investigation into Trump campaign associate Carter Page.[52]

President Reagan laid out his own vision for draining the Swamp in his time. In his 1981 inauguration address, he said:

We are a nation that has a government—not the other way around. And this makes us special among the nations of the earth. Our government has no power except that granted it by the people. It is time to check and reverse the growth of government, which shows signs of having grown beyond the consent of the governed.

It is my intention to curb the size and influence of the federal establishment and to demand recognition of the distinction between the powers granted to the federal government and those reserved to the states or to the people. All of us need to be reminded that the federal

51 https://www.whitehouse.gov/briefings-statements/the-inaugural-address/

52 https://www.nytimes.com/2020/08/14/us/politics/kevin-clinesmith-durham-investigation.html

government did not create the states; the states created the federal government.

Now, so there will be no misunderstanding, it's not my intention to do away with government. It is rather to make it work—work with us, not over us; to stand by our side, not ride on our back. Government can and must provide opportunity, not smother it; foster productivity, not stifle it.

If we look to the answer as to why for so many years we achieved so much, prospered as no other people on Earth, it was because here in this land we unleashed the energy and individual genius of man to a greater extent than has ever been done before. Freedom and the dignity of the individual have been more available and assured here than in any other place on Earth. The price for this freedom at times has been high, but we have never been unwilling to pay that price.[53]

Reagan, like Trump, knew that a small handful of people, the well-connected class—the Clintons, for example—should not rule the country. These people live in Georgetown; they live in the Acela corridor. But they don't understand true Americans like you and me. They don't work for a living—they steal from you for a living. When you expose the Swamp, their media allies come out with you—just consider how people like Peter Schweizer or James O'Keefe have been treated.[54] The Swamp protects their own with the help of their media allies at places like Media Matters and Vox.

---

[53] https://www.reaganlibrary.gov/research/speeches/inaugural-address-january-20-1981

[54] https://www.thedailybeast.com/peter-schweizer-who-smeared-hillary-clinton-is-back-for-joe-biden-dont-buy-it

In *Trump and Churchill: Defenders of Western Civilization,* I wrote:

> President Donald Trump is going to be a greater defender of Western civilization than Prime Minister Winston Churchill was. I admire both men, I see both as serving an incredibly important role in saving Western civilization. In no way do I seek to diminish Churchill's accomplishments. In fact, without Churchill, Trump may not have been able to do what he did. I believe Churchill's leadership against the Nazis and Soviet Union developed an important foreign policy handbook for dealing with threats to Western civilization, one that Trump has been able to replicate to defend Western civilization from its threats in the twenty-first century.

In this current book, I make a different claim: not only were both Reagan and Trump unlikely men to become president, but they became unlikely heroes—and they were heroes not only to lovers of freedom and liberty but to Americans at large. As I said previously, no experienced political commentator or high-paid consultant ever predicted that Trump or Reagan could become president—after all, they did not *want* Reagan or Trump to be their president.

Both men became presidents and heroes in the face of high-paid political consultants and the Establishment in both major political parties. Actually, "both major political parties" does not do their accomplishments justice; they overcame opposition and mockery from the Republican Party, the Democratic Party, the media party, the Beltway Swamp party, and so on.

They did it despite the fact that their backgrounds did not particularly point to a conservative presidency. After all, both were not even Republicans as young adults, or even in their later years before running for public office. But both came to their viewpoints the way that many people do: through experience, through careful thought, and through observation of what was going on around them.

Plenty of people have great ideas, but both Trump and Reagan had the ability to communicate their ideas and their reasons for those ideas in simple and clear language.

As you have no doubt gathered by now, numerous similarities exist between Trump and Reagan. In addition to exploring those similarities, this book provides analysis on how those similarities led to a reshaping of American politics and the betterment of American society and around the globe. Consider just a few more of those similarities now: both Reagan and Trump were mocked by the supposedly expert and sophisticated media—the graduates of Harvard, Yale, and other supposedly intellectual establishments. Late-night hosts and comedians piled on both men, thinking *they themselves* were the ones who represented most people. (In reality, they represented only the people they talked to on a regular basis—that is, those in upper Manhattan or Beverly Hills.)

Shortly after the death of Reagan in June 2004, Tim Graham praised Dinesh D'Souza's summary of the Reagan presidency. Graham wrote:

In the prologue to his book on Reagan Dinesh D'Souza captured the flavor of how Reagan was greeted by the Washington establishment. Everything Reagan sought to accomplish seemed ludicrous and uneducated to the long-standing liberal consensus. Tax cuts would be wildly inflationary. A foreign policy based on the radical notion that Communism should be put on the ash heap of history was dismissed as a bellicose fantasy too dangerous for the nuclear age. At the end of it all, Reagan was the wise man, and all his detractors—Democrats and ersatz Republicans, political scientists and economists, "Sovietologists" and journalists—were the dummies.[55]

Steven Hayward, author of *The Age of Reagan*, summarizes how the Democratic and Republican parties tried to stop Reagan from being a successful president, from the beginning of his presidency. Despite the fact that Reagan's 1980 landslide gave Republicans more power, "old establishment bulls were distinctly unenthusiastic about the new president," Hayward writes. Like Trump, who has faced down fake Republicans, RINOs (Republicans in name only), and has-beens like Senator Mitt Romney, Reagan faced down the weak-kneed old guard who wanted to be invited to as many cocktail parties and other Georgetown socials as possible, conservatism be damned.

Senators Bob Dole and Pete Domenici "laid repeated roadblocks in the path of Reagan's economic policy," Hayward writes, while Senator Mark Hatfield provided further intransigence by opposing Reagan's plan to "cut social spending, eliminate cabinet departments," and make the government suck less in general. The entrenched Establishment will always be in the pocket of the lobbyist class, the government shills, the PR machine. Better to tuck one's testicles into oneself than to stand up to entrenched interests and say no to a massive government;

---

[55] https://www.nationalreview.com/2004/06/reagan-vs-media-tim-graham/

Reagan found this out when he faced *Republicans* who were too weak and afraid to cut any sort of spending or even cut taxes!

President Reagan popularized the phrase "drain the Swamp," appointing the Grace Commission to investigate waste in the federal government.[56]

On receiving the final report of the Grace Commission, Reagan said:

> All of you are here today because of your deep concern about a problem in government that's easy to talk about in terms of saving billions of dollars a year. The war against waste and inefficiency is worth waging on just these grounds alone, but I know your involvement goes even beyond this. The people who came before us in this nation put a heavy emphasis on what is today almost a forgotten virtue. I remember back in Dixon, Illinois, when I was growing up, it was called thriftiness. Thriftiness was a quality appreciated as a kind of signal about the maturity and judgment of a person or institution, an indication that deeper values were there. Some of you in business have noticed that when a company gets in trouble, there are more serious problems than simple inefficiency—all sorts of projects and activities that are wasteful or marginal and a neglect of those products or services that made the firm successful in the first place.
>
> Well, government is no different. And as the people here know better than most, the federal government was headed a few years ago in much the same direction. It was neglecting essential tasks like protecting our nation's

---

[56]   https://www.reaganlibrary.gov/sites/default/files/archives/textual/topics/ppsscc.pdf

security abroad and upholding the law at home while it built gigantic bureaucracies to handle all sorts of problems, problems it was neither competent nor intended to handle. I used to use an example in some of my mashed-potato circuit days about the town that decided that they would have better traffic safety if they raised the height of their traffic signs and various warning signs from five feet above the ground to seven feet above the ground. And then, the federal government stepped in and said they had a department to come in and help them, and their plan was to lower the streets two feet.

Well, then these special interests became involved. Pretty soon the way to a prospering political career was to vote for higher appropriations and for grand, new spending schemes that appeal to this or that voting bloc. And if this pattern of putting politics over country sounds familiar, that's because it is. Historians have frequently seen in this "bread and circuses" climate the signs of government in decline and a nation in decay. Faith in our democratic system—and without that faith, democracy simply can't work—was being undermined. As James Madison said, "It's the gradual and silent encroachments of governments, not sudden revolutions, that prove to be the threat to freedom." So, it was the average citizen who harbored enormous feelings of resentment toward government and an enormous sense of frustration. They believed the only voices that were heard in this city were those of the organized lobbies or special interests, not the taxpayers.[57]

Likewise, President Trump faced his own opposition from the deep-state swamp monsters. The burrowed-in lifers in the

---

[57] https://www.reaganlibrary.gov/research/speeches/102885a

FBI and the CIA tried to take him down; consider the FBI's wasteful investigations into the fake Russian hoax and how they tried to ruin a good man, General Michael Flynn. They worked overtime, taking breaks only to commit affairs, to try to bring down Trump. Remember that these people get paid lots of money to supposedly prosecute federal crimes, but in reality they spend most of their time trying to halt conservative policies while racking up lucrative pension benefits paid for by you and me. They bite the hand that feeds them.

In the *Epoch Times*, a newspaper that does tremendous work in exposing the deep state, Roger Kimball wrote in May 2020 of the insidious Swamp and the fake hoaxes perpetuated by the disgraced FBI:

What started out as a solemn charge of treasonous collusion with the enemy to steal a presidential election gradually soured like milk left out in the sun. The team with the most megaphones kept shouting about felonious collusion with "the Russians" while they ran nightly cabarets replete with fictional Russian real estate deals and fictional Russian prostitutes.... [W]hat started with a suite of covert FBI investigations into Donald Trump and various members of his team even before Trump took office flowered into the fireworks of the Mueller investigation and then came to a pathetic, ignominious end when a confused and doddering Robert Mueller testified before Congress and, inter alia, claimed not to know what was Fusion GPS—the firm that hired the ex-spy Christopher Steele to produce the dossier that provided the impetus for Mueller's probe in the first place....

Flynn was an early casualty of President Barack Obama's deep-state attack on Trump. Fair-minded people have suspected he was set up since the indictment first came down. Now, we know.

There was no reason for the FBI to interview Flynn. He was a designated fall guy, set up by James Comey, Peter Strzok, and other high-ranking members of the establishment, because he would have been in a position to expose the larger "umbrella" operation of "Crossfire Hurricane," which began in July 2016, and whose aim was to delegitimize Trump and then, when that didn't work, to overturn the results of a free, open, and democratic presidential election.[58]

Kimball is right. Obama, one of the worst presidents this country has ever had, colluded with his minions to try to destroy President Trump's administration from the outset. *Hillary was supposed to win!* Remember, she had a 98 percent chance of winning!

The Democratic Party, which has a sad history, making its mark largely by slowing down efforts to end the disgusting practice of slavery, continues its sad, sad legacy by trying to undermine the will of millions of patriots across this country who voted for President Trump.

Consider likewise how the media establishment treated the presidency of Donald Trump. As noted previously both here and in *Trump and Churchill*, the mainstream media too despised Trump:

> [V]ery few newspapers endorsed Trump for president, which is a badge of honor, in that many in the media were very, very wrong about Trump.

---

[58] https://www.theepochtimes.com/flynn-revelations-may-lead-to-disillusionment-with-deep-state-not-retribution_3345884.html#comment_open

In fact, the newspapers that endorsed Trump reflected the small-town support for Trump. The newspapers include: the *Times-Gazette* (Hillsboro, Ohio; circulation of 4,300), the *Juneau Empire* (Juneau, Alaska; circulation of 7,500), and the *Waxahachie Daily Light* (Waxahachie, Texas; circulation of 3,191). But what did Trump care? He was speaking to the people and amassing free media coverage with every rally and tweet.

Trump and Reagan also were surprise heroes to social conservatives, to Christians. They stood up in the culture war while maintaining a respect for people of different opinions that allowed them to gain followers to the cause. Consider how Trump became the most pro-life, anti-abortion president in modern times since Reagan. Consider how he stood up for the biological reality that there are only two genders, male and female, even if his Supreme Court justices sometimes gave in to the desire to be toasted at Beltway cocktail parties instead of sticking to the truth.

And let's be honest, Trump was not supposed to be a hero to social conservatives. People like the great Jerry Falwell, the president of Liberty University, were mocked for endorsing Trump. But it's people like him who are getting the last laugh, as Trump continues to rack up praise from leading Christian and socially conservative groups.

Family Research Council (FRC) , a leading group among Christian conservatives, praised Trump for his decisions on gender issues (FRC, you may remember, was targeted by a gunman after the Southern Poverty Law Center put it on a "target list" for supporting traditional marriage.

In response to Trump's decision to no longer allow mentally ill people who think they're a different gender (sometimes called being transgender) to be armed with a weapon and put in high-stress military situations, FRC said:

> President Trump recognizes what the nation's military leadership and the American people realize, this Obama policy makes no sense. The last thing we should be doing is diverting billions of dollars from mission-critical training to something as controversial as gender reassignment surgery. However, the cost to readiness, recruitment, retention, morale, and cohesion would have been even greater under the Obama policy. As our nation faces serious national security threats, our troops shouldn't be forced to endure hours of transgender "sensitivity" classes and politically correct distractions like this one.[59]

In other words, making up your own genders is not brave!

Likewise, Susan B. Anthony List, a leading pro-life group, has summarized Trump's victories on defending preborn babies from slaughter in the womb at the hands of Planned Parenthood and the Democratic Establishment. (Note that members of the latter always say they care about black lives and then give hundreds of millions of dollars to the nation's largest abortion vendor so it can slaughter millions of black babies.) These victories include appointing pro-life judges, ending taxpayer funding of fetal-tissue research, and reinstating and expanding

---

[59] https://www.frc.org/newsroom/family-research-council-praises-president-trumps-decision-to-focus-on-military-priorities-over-obama-era-transgender-policy

the Mexico City policy, which blocks the use of American tax-payer money to fund international abortions.

On this particular victory, the group praises and explains the impact of Trump's decision:

President Trump not only reinstated the Mexico City policy, but expanded it to the new Protecting Life in Global Health Assistance program. This new policy ensures that our tax dollars are protected from funding the abortion industry overseas across *all* global health spending, not just family planning dollars. The Bush-era Mexico City policy protected roughly five hundred million dollars in spending—the new Trump policy protects over $8.8 billion overseas aid from funding abortion.[60]

Similarly, *National Review*'s Ramesh Ponnuru praised Trump in February 2020 for his record on defending the pre-born from abortion:

Since becoming president, Trump has done nearly everything that the pro-life movement has asked of him. Early in his term, he issued an executive order that blocked federal funds for family planning abroad from going to groups that advocate or perform abortion. Later, he issued another one blocking domestic family-planning money from going to such groups, which cut off a funding stream for Planned Parenthood. Other executive orders have imposed restrictions on funding for fetal-tissue research and attempted to protect the rights of pro-lifers in the medical field.[61]

He thanked Trump for appearing in person at the 2020 March for Life, the first U.S. president to ever do so:

---

[60] https://www.sba-list.org/trump-pro-life-wins
[61] https://www.nationalreview.com/magazine/2020/02/24/donald-trumps-pro-life-presidency/#slide-1

Conservatives often defend Trump by saying that what he does is better than what he says. But pro-lifers appreciate what he has said, too. Trump's speech at the march was a milestone: none of his predecessors had appeared there in person. When New York passed and other states considered legislation to ensure that abortion remained legal throughout pregnancy, Trump vigorously and vividly condemned the idea. Trump did distance himself from an Alabama law that attempts to ban abortion with no exceptions for rape and incest, exceptions that he supports. But pro-lifers have by and large not held that against him, since many of them considered the law a tactical mistake and most pro-life politicians have favored those exceptions.

Ponnuru, writing in a publication that has proven hostile to Trump, laid out what many social conservatives feel about Trump: he's become their unlikely hero. They weren't always so sure that he would be a good leader, but many took a chance on him because his opponent, Hillary Clinton, supported so many awful policies, like allowing abortion up until the moment of birth.[62] Trump famously pointed out during an October 2016 debate that Clinton wants to allow abortionists to "rip the baby out of the womb in the ninth month."

Furthermore, a *New York Times* article found that young voters were actually *more drawn* to Trump because of his pro-life stance.[63]

Michael Leaser of Charlemagne Institute explained why much of Middle America likes Trump: because he is pro-life!

---

62   https://www.vox.com/policy-and-politics/2016/10/19/13341464/
     trump-clinton-debate-abortion-question
63   https://www.nytimes.com/2020/05/06/us/politics/young-republicans-
     trump.html

Commenting on Trump's decision to speak at the March for Life, Leaser wrote:

By attending the seminal event that represents the primary social issue for his conservative base, Trump signals that he not only understands, but literally stands with, those seeking to make abortion illegal. At the rally, he touted his administration's decision to end federal spending for abortions overseas, the so-called Mexico City policy, which every Republican president has instituted since President Reagan. He also discussed his decision to end Title X funding, which offers funding for family planning services, for any group that performs (or refers for) abortion, effectively ending Title X funding for groups like Planned Parenthood.[64]

Courts later upheld Trump's smart cuts to abortion-vendor funding.[65] Trump also very smartly protected the conscience rights of pro-life doctors and nurses.[66]

So now that we have touched briefly on what the Swamp is and how Reagan and Trump shocked the country by winning the presidency, let us move on to the different ways they led and continued to surprise and win over supporters.

Reagan and Trump knew how to talk to people and win over crowds. It's one reason Reagan was called "The Great Communicator" and one reason many people like Trump.

As I wrote in *Trump and Churchill*, Trump shows an incredible ability to communicate to all people, using a variety of

---

[64] https://www.intellectualtakeout.org/article/why-does-middle-america-vote-trump/

[65] https://studentsforlife.org/2020/06/10/trump-administration-can-defund-planned-parenthood-of-title-x-dollars-federal-judge-rules/

[66] https://studentsforlife.org/2020/06/15/trump-administration-finalizes-rule-to-protect-conscience-rights-of-doctors/

techniques. I wrote that Twitter helped Trump become a great communicator because:

> ...having to reduce one's thoughts to 140 characters year after year is good training for becoming an effective communicator. Trump of course knows that much of his base, as is typical for a Republican politician, is middle-aged, married men and women. So what did Trump, whose genius for tabloids and media was shaped as a real estate developer and New York socialite, do? He merged the political ideology of his daughter and son-in-law, pushing criminal justice reform with an entity who is popular and well-known to Millennials: Kim Kardashian. Oh, and did you remember that Kim Kardashian's stepparent, who is transgender, supported Trump? And now the media is forced to cover Trump's middle-ground beliefs on trans-gender people with his criminal-justice-reform measure. I mean, Trump was able to turn someone famous for a sex tape into a serious political advocate and now law student. For bringing respectability to the Kardashian family once again, the man deserves a Nobel Peace Prize. That takes genius.

In another way, Trump and Reagan learned how to com-municate to people through consistent conversations and discussion with average Americans. Trump mastered this through his show *The Apprentice*, but also through regular appearances on Fox News' morning show *Fox & Friends*.

The website Vox, in of course a critical way of President Trump, nevertheless had to admit that Trump had mastered his appearances on *Fox & Friends*, appearing on the show regularly before and after winning the presidency, to share his views on a variety of issues:

Before Trump became the Republican nominee for president, Fox News had a somewhat adversarial relationship with Trump. He was an outsider, a former Democrat, a reality TV star—and not always good at getting in line with the Republican Party. In fact, one of his signature moments in the primary was taking down Jeb Bush, the establishment candidate.

> But *Fox & Friends* was always friendlier to Trump, a frequent caller to the show, and its coverage was a preview of how the rest of the network would evolve.

The show's hosts were always good at making Trump feel like they were on his side, but once he won the presidency, *Fox & Friends* ramped up this rhetoric, whether consciously or not.[67]

At the time Trump went on *Fox & Friends*, he was not even necessarily a Republican. However, true to his identity as an unlikely hero, he knew that many *Fox & Friends* listeners would want to hear what he had to say about issues such as the stock market, foreign policy, and trade.

Likewise, Reagan gained a substantial audience of blue-collar Americans by hosting over one thousand radio broadcasts from 1975 to 1979, the years leading up to his successful presidential run.[68] As noted by the Ronald Reagan Presidential Foundation:

---

[67] https://www.vox.com/2017/8/7/16083122/breakfast-club-fox-and-friends

[68] https://www.loc.gov/static/programs/national-recording-preservation-board/documents/ReaganOnRadio.pdf

In a daily radio commentary that ran from 1975 to 1979, former California governor Ronald Reagan used his considerable acting and broadcast talents to build his reputation as "The Great Communicator" and lay the groundwork for a successful presidential run in 1980. These radio commentaries also helped Reagan transition from a national public figure appreciated more for his acting ability than his political acumen into a serious political figure.

Reagan gave 1,027 of these addresses to an audience of twenty to thirty million listeners each week, interrupted only by his initial run for the White House in 1976. A researcher visiting the Reagan Library found that the former governor wrote at least 679 of the commentaries in longhand on yellow legal pads. The manuscripts are currently archived at the Ronald Reagan Presidential Library in California.

In these sharp-edged commentaries, Reagan laid out the political themes that would become all too familiar during his presidency as he banged the drum for what Lee Edwards of the Heritage Foundation has called "a vision of faith and freedom that would restore Americans' confidence in themselves and their country, reignite the nation's engines of economic progress, and initiate a winning policy in the Cold War."[69]

Conservatives, including Reagan and Rush Limbaugh, have been attacked by the fake news media for taking over the radio and utilizing it for their own benefit. Reagan skillfully used the radio to broadcast his views to millions of people, which helped him build a substantial following, similar to how Trump utilized

---

[69] https://www.loc.gov/static/programs/national-recording-preservation-board/documents/ReaganOnRadio.pdf

shows like *Fox & Friends* to win support among the middle class and average Americans.

Trump and Reagan both excelled as presidents, shocking even some of their supporters by the degree to which they excelled and flourished as presidents. In one area, economics, they had some of their biggest successes, even if they had different beliefs on some issues.

CHAPTER 2

BOOM TIME

"President Reagan speaks with the authority of a man who knows what he believes and who has shown that he will stand by his beliefs in good times and bad. He is no summer soldier of conservatism, but one who fought in the ranks when the going wasn't good. Again, that reassures even those who do not share those beliefs. For authority is the respect won from others by the calm exercise of deep conviction."

—Prime Minister Margaret Thatcher[70]

"Common sense told us that when you put a big tax on something, the people will produce less of it. So, we cut the people's tax rates, and the people produced more than ever before. The economy bloomed like a plant that had been cut back and could now grow quicker and stronger. Our economic program brought about the longest peacetime expansion in our history: real family income up, the poverty rate down, entrepreneurship booming, and an explosion in research and new technology. We're exporting more than

---

[70] https://www.margaretthatcher.org/document/107425

*ever because American industry because more competitive,
and at the same time, we summoned the national will to
knock down protectionist walls abroad instead of erecting
them at home."*

—President Ronald Reagan in
his farewell address[71]

*"In just three short years, we have shattered the mentality
of American decline, and we have rejected the downsizing
of America's destiny."*

—President Donald Trump[72]

President Trump deserves praise for the way he deregulated the markets while maintaining important pro-America protections already in place. Despite the fact that he was opposed by the Swamp monsters who want the status quo, who want unchecked, illegal immigration (God forbid they have to hire American workers!), Trump led an economic resurgence like no other; even now, as I write this, the economy is turning around in the face of the Chinese Communist Party's manufactured coronavirus crisis. He has taken on the Swamp and emerged as an unlikely hero to millions of Americans.

Consider some important successes of Trump's economic policies. A White House briefing notes:

► Real GDP growth under President Trump has beaten the Congressional Budget Office's (CBO) projections

---

[71] https://millercenter.org/the-presidency/presidential-speeches/
january-11-1989-farewell-address

[72] https://www.whitehouse.gov/briefings-statements/
historic-results-president-donald-j-trumps-economic-agenda/

every year and exceeded the rate of the Obama Administration's expansion....

▶ Unemployment rates for African Americans, Hispanic Americans, Asian Americans, Americans without a high school degree, and disabled Americans have logged record lows....

▶ Nearly 2.5 million Americans have been lifted out of poverty, including nearly 1.4 million children.

▶ The poverty rates for African Americans and Hispanic Americans hit new lows in 2018....

▶ "Real household wealth has increased by nearly twelve trillion dollars since the start of 2017.

▶ The president's historic efforts to cut costly regulations are projected to increase household incomes by $3,100 a year.[73]

It's not just the administration that (of course) says the economy is doing well thanks to Trump's leadership (including his getting out of the way and freeing the American entrepreneur). Consider these other endorsements of Trump's policies:

Economist Casey Mulligan wrote in January 2020:

> The myriad deregulatory actions of the Trump administration are generating considerable cost savings, savings that even conservative critics of regulatory overreach are underestimating. Like the Grand Canyon, the vast scale of these deregulatory efforts (and their results) is hard to fathom.

---

[73]   https://www.whitehouse.gov/briefings-statements/historic-results-president-donald-j-trumps-economic-agenda/

In just three years the administration has reversed hundreds of regulations, many of which drone on for hundreds of pages. And it's done so without fear or favor. Many of the regulations reversed had been written and implemented at the behest of special interests, including large banks, trial lawyers, major health insurance companies, big tech companies, labor unions, and foreign drug manufacturers.[74]

Furthermore, a report by the Council of Economic Advisors found:

> Since 2017, consumers and small businesses have been able to live and work with more choice and less federal government interference. They can purchase health insurance in groups or as individuals without paying for categories of coverage that they do not want or need. Small businesses can design compensation packages that meet the needs of their employees, enter into a genuine franchise relationship with a larger corporation, or seek confidential professional advice on the organization of their workplaces. Consumers have a variety of choices as to less expensive wireless and wired internet access. Small banks are no longer treated as "too big to fail" (they never were) and subject to the costly regulatory scrutiny that goes with that designation.[75]

I strongly believe that Trump came to his beliefs about the Swamp, overregulation, and markets through his tremendous work as a real estate developer in New York. One of his greatest

---

74 https://economics21.org/trump-deregulation-unnoticed-experts
75 https://www.whitehouse.gov/wp-content/uploads/2019/06/The-Economic-Effects-of-Federal-Deregulation-Interim-Report.pdf

strengths is taking in new information, processing it, and then applying it to his life and political beliefs.

I reiterate now what I wrote in *Trump and Churchill*:

> Let's start with how Trump is a genius.
>
> For all the criticism that Trump is obtuse or lacks social grace, he has an incredibly amount of interpersonal or emotional intelligence. You don't become the greatest developer in the New York real estate market by being a quiet fellow who works from nine a.m. to five p.m. You become the greatest real estate developer by working long hours, but also getting to know the people working for you and your clients. Trump is known to talk to everyone working for him as well as his guests. The laborer, the foreman, the bellhop. He does this first of all because he is a genuine guy and treats the little guy with respect. But he also does this because this is how he acquires the necessary knowledge to make decisions. Like the detective who becomes best friends with a local bartender, Trump knows who has the knowledge that others may not have or that others may not tell him.
>
> The day laborer who is being sent home early every day is able to tell Trump, explicitly or not, that the supervisor isn't planning out the construction schedule well, so people are running out of work to do during the day. The bellhop hears the complaints, or compliments, about guests' stays at a hotel while he is helping them pack up their cab to head to the airport, and can relay that information to Trump so changes can be made.

Likewise, Reagan's economic agenda led to an economic boom, inspiring optimism particularly on the heels of the weak,

annual real GDP growth of 3.5 percent—4.9 percent after the recession. In inflation-adjusted 2009 dollars, GDP jumped from 6.5 trillion at the end of 1980 to 8.61 trillion at the end of 1988. That's a 32 percent bump.

But it's not just the upper class and wealthy that benefitted under Reagan: "Real (inflation-adjusted) median household income shot up some 10 percent in the Reagan years."

These statistics are backed up by neutral sources including the Bureau of Labor Statistics and numerous nonpartisan economic reports. An economic analysis by the libertarian Cato Institute described the following successes of Reagan's economic leadership:

▶ Real economic growth averaged 3.2 percent during the Reagan years versus 2.8 percent during the Ford-Carter years and 2.1 percent during the Bush-Clinton years.

▶ Real median family income grew by four thousand dollars during the Reagan period after experiencing no growth in the pre-Reagan years; it experienced a loss of almost $1,500 in the post-Reagan years.

▶ Interest rates, inflation, and unemployment fell faster under Reagan than they did immediately before or after his presidency.[78]

In his own words, describing his economic plan, Reagan laid out a bold agenda to free the American worker and put freedom back into the hands of the American people. In a magnificent

---

[78] https://www.cato.org/publications/policy-analysis/supplyside-tax-cuts-truth-about-reagan-economic-record

speech shortly after he survived an assassination attempt, he said:

> Let us cut through the fog for a moment. The answer to a government that's too big is to stop feeding its growth. Government spending has been growing faster than the economy itself. The massive national debt which we accumulated is the result of the government's high spending diet. Well, it's time to change the diet and to change it in the right way.

This is an excellent idea. Government must stop growing! He continued:

> Reducing the growth of spending, cutting marginal tax rates, providing relief from overregulation, and following a noninflationary and predictable monetary policy are interwoven measures which will ensure that we have addressed each of the severe dislocations which threaten our economic future. These policies will make our economy stronger..."[79]

As president, Reagan helped free the American economy so jobs could grow and people could prosper. Unlike the leftist Democratic Party, which always finds government to be the solution, Reagan knew that the best thing government could do was get out of the way. It's simple. Cut spending. Cut taxes. Slash regulations. Let people prosper. Rinse and repeat.

He learned these lessons while touring the country for General Electric. While touring factories, he met the many men and women who were keeping America running and keeping

---

[79] https://www.reaganfoundation.org/media/128629/congress.pdf

the lights on. He knew that any economic agenda should serve American workers first, and not try to enrich globalist elites and big banks. He realized that what matters first is the American people.

Praising legal immigrants, Reagan said things that you will never hear from people like Obama or Bernie Sanders:

> These families came here to work. They came to build. Others came to America in different ways, from other lands, under different, and often harrowing conditions. But this place symbolizes what they all managed to build, no matter where they came from or how they came or how much they suffered. They helped to build that magnificent city across the river. They spread across the land, building other cities and other towns and incredibly productive farms.

But they didn't just come here to make it for themselves, Reagan argued; they came here because they wanted a better country. They were true patriots. He continued:

> They came to make America work. They didn't ask what this country could do for them but what they could do to make this—this refuge the greatest home of freedom in history. They brought with them courage, ambition and the values of family, neighborhood, work, peace, and freedom. We all came from different lands but we share the same values, the same dream.[80]

---

[80] https://www.americanrhetoric.com/speeches/ronaldreaganlibertyp-ark.htm

These are the people we should reward and build up, which both Reagan and Trump recognized.

Trade

However, on trade, President Reagan made some mistakes, including not being strong enough on protecting American interests in his trade deals. For example, he helped lay the groundwork for the disastrous North American Free Trade Agreement, or NAFTA. While NAFTA had some benefits, the drafters, deliberately or not, failed to ensure proper protections for workers, which led to a hollowing out of manufacturing jobs in the United States.

Reagan said in 1988:

> Our peaceful trading partners are not our enemies. They are our allies. We should beware of the demagogues who are ready to declare a trade war against our friends, weakening our economy, our national security, and the entire free world. All while cynically waving the American flag. The expansion of the international economy is not a foreign invasion; it is an American triumph, one we worked hard to achieve, and something central to our vision of a peaceful and prosperous world of freedom.[81]

Reagan was *correct* in saying that peaceful trading partners are not our enemies, but many times trade is not peaceful. China regularly rips off our great American workers and entrepreneurs by stealing their intellectual property or jobs.

---

[81]   https://www.aei.org/carpe-diem/if-trump-aspires-to-be-ronald-reagan-he-should-pay-close-attention-to-reagans-1988-radio-address-on-free-trade/

He unfortunately was a weak leader on this issue, unlike Trump. Trump has been a strong hawk on putting numerous sanctions and tariffs on China, and on using the bully pulpit to hold China accountable.[82]

And he is right to do so, especially considering how China regularly rips off our great American workers and industry by stealing from us, as noted above, and trying to wage economic warfare against us!

Trump stated on the reform of our trade policies with Canada and Mexico:

> The USMCA [United States-Mexico-Canada Agreement] is the largest, fairest, most balanced, and modern trade agreement ever achieved. There's never been anything like it. Other countries are now looking at it, but there can't be a border like that because, believe it or not, that is by far the biggest border anywhere in the world, in terms of economy, in terms of people. There's nothing even close. The USMCA is estimated to add another 1.2 percent to our GDP and create countless new American jobs. It will make our blue-collar boom—which is beyond anybody's expectation—even bigger, stronger, and more extraordinary, delivering massive gains for the loyal citizens of our nation.

For the first time in American history, we have replaced a disastrous trade deal that rewarded outsourcing with a truly fair

---

[82] https://www.whitehouse.gov/briefings-statements/remarks-president-trump-actions-china/

and reciprocal trade deal that will keep jobs, wealth, and growth right here in America.[83]

In 2018, the White House Office of Trade and Manufacturing Policy released a thirty-six-page report that details some of the ways that China tries to interfere in our market economy and our industrial manufacturing enterprises. It opens by noting:

> The People's Republic of China (China) has experienced rapid economic growth to become the world's second largest economy while modernizing its industrial base and moving up the global value chain. However, much of this growth has been achieved in significant part through aggressive acts, policies, and practices that fall outside of global norms and rules (collectively, "economic aggression"). Given the size of China's economy and the extent of its market-distorting policies, China's economic aggression now threatens not only the U.S. economy but also the global economy as a whole.[84]

The report identified six areas where China threatens the United States through economic aggression.

It said that China works to "protect China's home market from import and competition" and to "expand China's share of global markets." It also noted that China is working to expand its control of global natural resources, dominate manufacturing, acquire technologies and intellectual properties (read:

---

[83] https://www.whitehouse.gov/briefings-statements/remarks-president-trump-signing-ceremony-united-states-mexico-canada-trade-agreement/

[84] https://www.whitehouse.gov/wp-content/uploads/2018/06/FINAL-China-Technology-Report-6.18.18-PDF.pdf

steal), and "capture" high-level tech for economic and military reasons.

Addressing the need to bring jobs and factories back to the U.S., Trump said in an August 2020 speech:

> As we celebrate Whirlpool's 109-year legacy of American manufacturing excellence, today I want to lay out my vision to bring millions and millions more jobs and thousands more factories back to American shores where they belong. We've been doing it long and hard. One of the reasons you're successful today happens to be a meeting I had probably four years ago with a very good representative of your company, saying what they were doing to you and how badly you were being treated by other countries. And you know what I did. And here we are today, the most successful plant. And we've done this in a lot of places.

The Office of Trade and Manufacturing Policy report concluded:

> Given the size of China's economy, the demonstrable extent of its market-distorting policies, and China's stated intent to dominate the industries of the future, China's acts, policies, and practices of economic aggression now targeting the technologies and IP of the world threaten not only the U.S. economy but also the global innovation system as a whole.

President Trump regularly projected optimism in his speeches. At a speech to the Economic Club of New York in November 2019, he declared the success of his economic agenda, predicated on getting the government out of the way:

In 2016, I stood before you supremely confident in what our people could achieve if government stopped punishing American workers and started promoting American workers and American companies. Our middle class was being crushed under the weight of a punitive tax code, oppressive regulations, one-sided trade deals, and an economic policy that put America's interest last, and a very deep last at that.

I knew that if we lifted these burdens from our economy, and unleashed our people to pursue their ambitions and realize their limitless potential, then economic prosperity would come thundering back to our country at a record speed. And that's what's happening.[85]

Even though the coronavirus crisis, manufactured by the Chinese Communist Party, has put a dent in the economic gains, our economy is still strong and in a good place because of President Trump's leadership. It's the same type of leadership in the face of a sluggish economy, which he inherited from President Obama's weak leadership, that President Reagan showed when he took over from President Carter.

Many conservatives were skeptical of Trump as a candidate, but he has shown them that he understands the benefits of limited government and freedom. They were skeptical of his views on property rights and on trade, for example. But at the end of the day, Trump turned out to be one of the greatest champions of economic freedom that the country has ever had. He came in and slashed taxes and regulations. He protected American workers and stood up for entrepreneurs.

---

[85] https://www.whitehouse.gov/briefings-statements/remarks-president-trump-economic-club-new-york-new-york-ny/

Consider groups like the Club for Growth, which publicly opposed and engaged in a spat with Trump when he was a candidate. It has since warmed up to Trump, and supported him in 2020.

As the news website The Hill reported:

> The Club for Growth joins a string of Republican lawmakers and conservative advocacy groups who were once fiercely critical of Trump but have since warmed to him. Trump is the unquestioned GOP leader, and Republicans who oppose him have been elected out of office, exited Washington of their own accord or seen their fundraising and political influence dry up. [Club for Growth president David] McIntosh does not see a conflict in the change of course, pointing to Trump's tax cuts and deregulatory efforts as in line with the Club for Growth's mission."[86]

Notably, Club for Growth spent millions in 2016 trying to defeat candidate Trump!

Trump's economic policies make the radical socialists, the central planners, the busybody politicians *furious*. They want as many people dependent on welfare as possible. They want to destroy American capitalism so that people will turn to *them* and give them more money. They hate freedom.

What Americans needed in Trump, they received. They needed a president who would stand up to the *New York Times*, the race hustlers, the lobbyist class and say no. They wanted someone who would stand up for our hardworking law

---

[86] https://thehill.com/homenews/campaign/454636-club-for-growth-warms-to-trump-after-2016-fight

enforcement officers, our courageous entrepreneurs who risk their livelihood to provide economic opportunities, and faithful religious people. They were sick of being demonized by Obama, who tried to ruin an order of Catholic nuns who cared for poor people. They knew Obama was antagonistic to any religious group that didn't endorse transgenderism, abortion, and homosexual marriage. They saw that Trump *respected* their religious beliefs.[87]

Taxation

Like Trump, Reagan faced criticism over his pro-freedom economic agenda. It's hard to believe now, but there was a time when even the Republican Party was skeptical of tax cuts. However, Reagan pushed ahead and lowered taxes through his supply-side economics plan, championed by economist Arthur Laffer. While Establishment hacks and big government socialists try to say the tax cuts did not work, because they don't trust you and me to keep our own money, the evidence is clear: Reagan's tax cuts helped accelerate the American economy.

Daniel Mitchell, an economist at the Heritage Foundation, concluded in a 2001 article:

> President Ronald Reagan's record includes sweeping economic reforms and deep across-the-board tax cuts, market deregulation, and sound monetary policies to contain inflation. His policies resulted in the largest

---

[87]   https://www.supremecourt.gov/opinions/19pdf/19-431_5i36.pdf

peacetime economic boom in American history and nearly thirty-five million more jobs.[88]

He also noted:

Many critics of reducing taxes claim that the Reagan tax cuts drained the U.S. Treasury. The reality is that federal revenues increased significantly between 1980 and 1990:

▶ Total federal revenues doubled from just over $517 billion in 1980 to more than $1 trillion in 1990. In constant inflation-adjusted dollars, this was a 28 percent increase in revenue.

▶ As a percentage of the gross domestic product (GDP), federal revenues declined only slightly from 18.9 percent in 1980 to 18 percent in 1990.

▶ Revenues from individual income taxes climbed from just over $244 billion in 1980 to nearly $467 billion in 1990. In inflation-adjusted dollars, this amounts to a 25 percent increase.

Like Reagan, Trump took bold action on taxation, solidifying his reputation as a tax cutter even though he had previously supported raising taxes. In 2017, he boldly pushed through massive income and corporate tax cuts, helping the fiery-hot economy burn even hotter.[89]

For his bold action, Trump drew a wide array of praise, and many companies quickly offered one-thousand-dollar bonuses and other benefits to workers after the tax cut and job growth legislation was passed in December 2017.

---

[88] https://www.heritage.org/taxes/report/the-real-reagan-economic-record-responsible-and-successful-fiscal-policy

[89] https://www.congress.gov/115/bills/hr1/BILLS-115hr1enr.pdf

The leftist *USA Today* had to admit the benefits of the tax cuts:

> A growing number of companies benefiting from tax cuts are showing their employees the money. One-time cash bonuses are the most popular way companies are sharing the windfall they expect from paying less in taxes. Many employers are boosting hourly pay. And a small number say they will increase matching contributions to workers' 401(k) plans.
>
> Walmart is the latest to join their ranks. The retail giant has announced Thursday it plans to boost the starting pay for hourly workers to eleven dollars and pay up to one thousand dollars in a one-time cash bonus to eligible associates based on seniority.[90]
>
> Americans for Tax Reform compiled a longer list of benefits, including the following bonuses and raises that went to workers, many of whom were low-income and middle-income.[91] Its list includes "1,100 examples of small business expansion, new hires, pay raises, Opportunity Zone job creation, and utility rate reductions where the GOP-enacted Tax Cuts and Jobs Act was cited as a key factor."

For example, Americans for Tax Reform announced these victories in Michigan:

> Every income group in every Michigan congressional district saw a tax cut.

---

[90] https://www.usatoday.com/story/money/2018/01/11/list-companies-paid-bonuses-boosted-pay-since-tax-bill-passed/1023848001/

[91] https://www.atr.org/list

Doubled child tax credit: 647,610 Michigan households are benefiting from the TCJA's doubling of the child tax credit.

Standard deduction: At least 3,463,240 Michigan households are benefiting from the TCJA's doubling of the standard deduction.

Obamacare individual mandate tax relief: 147,340 Michigan households are no longer stuck paying the much-loathed Obamacare individual mandate tax, thanks to the TCJA's elimination of this penalty. Eight-two percent of Michigan households hit with this tax made less than fifty thousand dollars per year.

Lower utility bills: As a direct result of the TCJA's corporate rate cut, Michiganders are paying lower utility bills. Lower electric, water, and gas bills help households each month, and also help small businesses operating on slim profit margins.

But it's not just blue-collar, Midwestern states that benefitted. Even leftist, Trump-hating states like California benefitted. Americans for Tax Reform reported:

2,649,200 California households are benefiting from the TCJA's doubling of the child tax credit.

Every income group in every California congressional district received a tax cut. Nationwide, a typical family of four received a $2,000 annual tax cut and a single parent with one child received a $1,300 annual tax cut.

11,633,710 California households are benefiting from the TCJA's doubling of the standard deduction. Thanks to the tax cuts, nine out of ten households take the standard deduction which provides tax relief and simplifies the tax filing process.

553,000 California households are benefiting from the TCJA's elimination of the Obamacare individual mandate tax. Most households hit with this tax made less than $50,000 per year.

Lower utility bills: As a direct result of the TCJA's corporate tax rate cut, California residents are saving money on utility bills. Lower electric, water, and gas bills help households and small businesses operating on tight margins. California utilities that have passed along tax savings include—but are not limited to—California Water Service and Pacific Gas and Electric Company....

Thanks to the tax cuts, California businesses of all sizes are hiring, expanding, raising pay and increasing employee benefits.

Before the legislation passed, Trump laid out his agenda in support of growing the economy through aggressive tax cuts at a speech in Missouri. It received widespread praise from his own party, something that Reagan struggled with regarding some of his tax cuts.

According to the White House, the following people, in addition to Trump's Cabinet members, praised his genius and economic intelligence.[92]

Senator Roy Blunt (Republican from Missouri) said: "As President Trump made clear today, fixing our broken tax code is about two things: helping hardworking Missouri families keep more of what they earn and ensuring there

[92] https://www.whitehouse.gov/briefings-statements/praise-president-trumps-tax-reform-speech-missouri/

are more opportunities and better-paying jobs for every American. I've heard from countless Missouri families, small-business owners, and manufacturers about the challenges they face with our outdated tax code. They need relief, and I appreciate President Trump's push to make sure they get it."

Representative Blaine Luetkemeyer (Republican from Missouri): "Americans work too hard and produce too many great products to have our economy weighed down by outdated laws and elected officials who lack the courage to make tough decisions. It is incredible to have President Trump visit the Third Congressional District during this historic week. With all eyes on the Senate now, it is my sincere hope they join the House in passing meaningful reform so we can soon deliver a bill to the president's desk."

Representative Vicky Hartzler (Republican from Missouri): "It's an honor to accompany President Trump on his trip and welcome him to my home state. Americans are ready for a change in the tax code that allows them to flourish instead of just get by. The Tax Cuts and Jobs Act would do just that by roughly doubling the standard deduction, which 71 percent of Missourians currently use. I look forward to continuing to work with President Trump and my colleagues in the Senate to bring Missourians and the American people much-needed relief."

Representative Jason Smith (Republican from Missouri): "President Trump knows that tax cuts for the folks in Missouri will unleash the economy and are [for] the people that he's trying to help the most, and it's nice to have him back in our state."

In other words, Trump won over the representatives of Missouri and ultimately helped push through his tax cuts. He showed the American workers and the American people that he supported them, and in doing so, won over more supporters. The least partisan things should be jobs and other opportunities to earn a living, provide for a family, and save for retirement.

President Reagan and President Trump took on the Swamp and pushed through a strong agenda of deregulation and economic freedom. Reagan stared down the air traffic controllers' union and reminded bureaucrats that they work for the American people, not the other way around.

As Politico conceded:

> On this day in 1981, President Ronald Reagan fired more than eleven thousand air traffic controllers who had ignored his order to return to work. The sweeping mass firing of federal employees slowed commercial air travel, but it did not cripple the system as the strikers had forecast.
>
> Two days earlier, nearly thirteen thousand controllers walked out after contract talks with the Federal Aviation Administration collapsed. As a result, some seven thousand flights across the country were canceled on that day at the peak of the summer travel season."[93]

Taking on the Swamp and pushing for economic freedom takes courage. A former union man, Reagan became an unlikely hero by taking on the air traffic controllers. Both Reagan and Trump also turned out to be champions to social conservatives and Christians.

CHAPTER 3

UNLIKELY HEROES

"I chose Mr. Trump because the alternative was the radically pro-abortion Hillary Clinton, and too many lives were at stake. We'd come too close to changing our generation's view on abortion; we couldn't let our courts be overtaken by judges who are in the pockets of the abortion industry.

"So I voted for Mr. Trump, and he has upheld his pro-life promises. I now believe that he will go down in history as the president who did the most to advance the cause of ending legal abortion."

—Kristan Hawkins, president,
Students for Life of America[94]

"Some see this simply as political advocacy; we see it as advocacy of spiritual and moral imperatives to protect life, freedom, family, justice, equality, civil rights, and peace."

—Father Frank Pavone and Alveda King,
niece of Martin Luther King Jr.[95]

---

[94] https://www.post-gazette.com/opinion/Op-Ed/2019/02/08/I-now-wear-a-MAGA-hat/stories/201902080042

"President Trump's leadership as the most effective pro-life president in American history has been a game-changer. As evidenced in his historic address at this year's March for Life, he has truly embraced our movement and delivered on his promise to be a pro-life president.... President Trump's support for life pervades his administration and his policies. He is unwavering in defense of the unborn, and he has put his words into action."

—Marjorie Dannenfelser, president, Susan B. Anthony List[96]

"I've noticed that everyone who is for abortion has already been born."

—President Ronald Reagan[97]

If you want to not make great friends at a D.C. or New York dinner party, bring up topics like abortion, gender, and religious liberty. The D.C. dinner party crowd looks down on Middle Americans who don't want to see Planned Parenthood receive over half a billion dollars a year from taxpayers like them. It looks down on people who don't want grown men using the same bathrooms as their young daughters. It looks down on anyone who doesn't immediately accept the new left-wing social engineering of the day. But President Reagan and President Trump bucked the D.C and New York left-wing Establishment, as well as the fake social conservatives in the GOP Establishment. They knew that if you want to win the culture war, you have to actually fight.

---

[96] https://www.foxnews.com/opinion/marjorie-dannenfelser-trump-most-pro-life-president-in-history-these-policies-a-game-changer

[97] https://www.goodreads.com/quotes/116615-i-ve-noticed-that-every-one-who-is-for-abortion-has-already

need people. And employers are hiring prisoners, and they would have never done it, except for what we've done with criminal justice reform—but even before that, because the economy has become so powerful.[104]

Father Frank Pavone concluded in a column for the website Newsmax:

> He translates beliefs—his and ours—into action that benefits us, our children, and our children's children. We are convinced that the church, and believers everywhere, should be able to recognize this kind of leadership, express their gratitude for it, and support our leaders when they support and defend, in concrete action, the faith and values the Gospel embodies.

On the issue of abortion, Reagan made changes similar to those of Trump, who was once pro-choice. Reagan signed, and then later regretted, one of the first pro-choice laws in the country while governor of California. He then spent the rest of his political life looking to undo that damage.

Reagan consistently spoke out in defense of the preborn. In fact, he wrote a book *while in the White House* about why we must abolish abortion. *Abortion and the Conscience of the Nation* was at the time the only book to be published by a sitting U.S. president.

Reagan was the first U.S. president to institute a federal ban on using taxpayer dollars to fund overseas abortions, a policy commonly known as the Mexico City policy.

---

[104] https://www.whitehouse.gov/briefings-statements/remarks-president-trump-68th-annual-national-prayer-breakfast/

The conservative Witherspoon Institute described the policy thus:

> In 1984, the Reagan administration outlined this pro-life policy during a UN conference on population and development in Mexico. It prevents any U.S. foreign assistance from funding groups that perform and promote abortions. It is effective, self-enforcing, and does not cost taxpayers a dime. All it requires is that groups receiving U.S. foreign aid sign an agreement not to promote or perform abortions.[105]

Reagan also supported ending all taxpayer funding of abortions, including supporting making the Hyde Amendment permanent. The Hyde Amendment forbids federal taxpayer dollars from being used by Medicaid to pay for abortions.

In a 1988 statement to Congress, Reagan wrote:

> The bill I am sending you has been named the "President's Pro-Life Act of 1988" to emphasize the urgent need to reduce the number of abortions in this country and to reaffirm life's sacred position in our Nation. The findings that would underlie the mandate of the statute point out that abortion takes the life of a living human being, that there is no right to abortion secured by the Constitution, and that the Supreme Court erred in its decision in Roe v. Wade in failing to recognize the humanity of the unborn child.

The key provision of the bill would enact, on a permanent and government-wide basis, the anti-abortion provision—commonly known as the Hyde Amendment—that is included annually in the appropriation act for the Department of Health

---

[105] https://www.thepublicdiscourse.com/2017/05/19416/

and Human Services. Enacting this prohibition on the funding of abortion in general legislation will extend its application to all agencies and to all Federal funds.[106]

In other words, Reagan didn't just say he was pro-life—he actually advocated for pro-life policies while in office (in addition to being an adoptive father himself). In the last months of his presidency, the Christian Science Monitor wrote this tribute to Reagan's record on life: "He has been an all-time champion of the right-to-life movement. With his friend and political colleague Attorney General Edwin Meese III at his side, Reagan proposed a spate of litigation and legislation that would have pulled the reins on abortion."[107]

The column also noted Reagan's championing of a policy that forbade family planning dollars from going to abortion vendors. That policy was held up in the courts for years but was eventually allowed to stand by the Supreme Court, and then was finally revived by President Trump after Establishment politicians like George H. W. Bush, Bill Clinton, and George W. Bush failed to enact it.[108]

Fittingly, President Trump reenacted that policy as the Protect Life Rule, which experts say could likely prevents numerous abortions.[109] Writing in the *Washington Examiner*, pro-life professor Michael New praised the decision by Trump:

> [T]he Trump administration's Protect Life Rule will likely improve public health outcomes. The Protect Life Rule

---

[106] https://www.reaganlibrary.gov/research/speeches/060888b
[107] https://www.csmonitor.com/1988/0728/dcurt28.html
[108] https://www.oyez.org/cases/1990/89-1391
[109] https://www.hhs.gov/about/news/2020/01/23/trump-admin-actions-to-protect-life-and-conscience-factsheet-released-01-23-20.html

does not cut any funds from family planning programs. Title X funds would still be available to thousands of Federally Qualified Health Centers (FQHCs), which offer a much wider range of healthcare services. Unlike Planned Parenthood clinics, for example, FQHCs offer mammograms. They also see far more prenatal patients and conduct more cervical cancer screenings....

Taxpayers should not have to subsidize abortion. Defunding facilities that perform abortions is an important policy goal for pro-lifers and taxpayers generally. In addition to the Protect Life Rule, Trump has strengthened the Mexico City policy, ensuring that taxpayers are not subsidizing organizations that promote or perform abortions overseas. Even though Title X funds did not directly pay for abortions, money is fungible, and these funds subsidized abortion procedures and promotion indirectly. Furthermore, a significant body of academic research shows that subsidizing abortions increases abortion rates. Overall, Planned Parenthood is America's number-one abortion provider, ending the lives of over 320,000 innocent unborn children every year. The Trump administration's Protect Life Rule is a key first step toward eliminating all taxpayer funding of organizations that profit from abortion.[110]

At the 1988 march for Life, Reagan spoke on the sacredness of human life:

Are we to forget the entire moral mission of our nation through its history? Well, my answer, and I know it's yours, is no. America was founded on a moral proposition that

---

[110] https://www.washingtonexaminer.com/opinion/op-eds/the-trump-administrations-protect-life-rule-is-a-win-for-women

Supreme Court, filling 30 percent of its seats with hand-picked conservatives.[115]

Many conservatives were worried about Trump's judicial picks, including people like Senator Ted Cruz, but in the end, Trump came out with victories and became a hero to conservatives.

CHAPTER 4

THE HATERS

"You're fighting against an oppressive left-wing ideology that is driven by hate and seeks to purge all dissent. And you understand that. Amazing at that age. You're young people, generally. A couple of oldsters out there—friends of mine. The radical left demands absolute conformity from every professor, researcher, reporter, journalist, corporation, entertainer, politician, campus speaker, and private citizen."

—President Donald Trump in an address
to Turning Point USA attendees[116]

Both Reagan and Trump were despised by the media, the Establishment, and the Swamp. Of course, if you tell this to your liberal friend, he will say that conservatives always complain about liberal bias but that the truth has a liberal bias.

However, numerous studies confirm that the media has a liberal bias. Consider the following:

A 2018 article on the website Investor's Business Daily noted that just 8 percent of the mainstream media's coverage of President Trump was positive, while 92 percent was negative. This was during a booming economy when the GDP was up and unemployment was down.[117]

A 2020 article in the *Boston Herald* noted: "Rich Noyes of the Media Research Center found that from March 4 (when Joe Biden had basically wrapped up the Democratic nomination) through May 31, Trump coverage on the ABC, CBS, and NBC evening newscasts was 94 percent negative. In May, it was 99.5 percent negative, an all-time low."[118]

Even the *Washington Post* felt the need to cover the issue, with a 2017 op-ed noting that 91 percent of media coverage of President Trump was negative.[119]

It's no wonder that many Americans, including Democrats, say that their trust in the media is low.[120]

Even the left-wing publication *The Nation* had to admit that Trump's criticism of the deep state was valid. Jeet Heer wrote in 2019:

> This full-throttle enthusiasm for unelected government officials, including the spies at the CIA, should give us pause.... This administrative state is often successful in coopting even presidential Cabinet members and parts of the White House staff, since they all receive institutional instruction from an army of nonappointed staffers.

---

[117] https://www.investors.com/politics/editorials/media-trump-hatred-coverage/

[118] https://www.bostonherald.com/2020/06/15/media-ups-the-ante-on-negative-coverage-of-trump/

[119] https://www.washingtonpost.com/blogs/erik-wemple/wp/2017/09/12/study-91-percent-of-recent-network-trump-coverage-has-been-negative/

[120] https://morningconsult.com/2020/04/22/media-credibility-cable-news-poll/

Trump isn't the first president to clash with the administrative state. The permanent bureaucracy has a bias toward the status quo, so any ambitious agenda, especially in foreign policy, often meets resistance. Richard Nixon and Henry Kissinger famously had to keep the Pentagon and National Security Council out of the loop as they created a back channel to the People's Republic of China. More recently, Barack Obama often felt hemmed in by the administrative state, believing it was trying to tie his hands in the Middle East with a bigger Syrian intervention than he wanted and also creating roadblocks to the Iran nuclear deal. As with Nixon, Obama found ways to work around the preferences of bureaucracy.[121]

In his 2015 kickoff speech, Trump said:

So now ISIS has the oil, and what they don't have, Iran has...and I will tell you this, and I said it very strongly, years ago, I said—and I love the military, and I want to have the strongest military that we've ever had, and we need it more now than ever—but I said, "Don't hit Iraq, because you're going to totally destabilize the Middle East." Iran is going to take over the Middle East, Iran and somebody else will get the oil, and it turned out that Iran is now taking over Iraq. Think of it. Iran is taking over Iraq, and they're taking it over big-league.

We spent two trillion dollars in Iraq, two trillion dollars. We lost thousands of lives, thousands in Iraq. We have wounded soldiers, who I love, I love—they're great— all over the place, thousands and thousands of wounded soldiers. And we have nothing. We can't even go there. We

---

[121]   https://www.thenation.com/article/archive/trump-deep-state/

But I can separate his personal flaws and unpresidential manners from what he's been accomplishing in Washington—cutting taxes, boosting the economy, creating jobs, etc. with no help from Democrats and too little help from many Republicans.

I don't know any other human in politics who could have withstood the bipartisan onslaught of hate that President Trump has and still be able to walk around with his head high and a smile on his face."[131]

While many in the media believe that the media looked kindly on Ronald Reagan, that is up for debate. In some ways, the media probably did treat Reagan better than they treated Trump, but that is not entirely clear.

Journalist Howard Kurtz said in 2004, when Reagan died, "The uplifting tone with which journalists are eulogizing Ronald Reagan is obscuring a central fact of his presidency: he had a very contentious relationship with the press."[132]

In assessing the media's coverage, let's again turn to the Media Research Center. While clearly conservative, the group relies heavily on objective, replicable data, such as time allocated to specific topics.

Heading into 2011, a hundred years after Reagan was born, the Media Research Center compiled numerous examples of the way the media covered Reagan, in anticipation of a cheerful rewrite of the media's bias toward him. It wrote in its summary:

---

[131] https://apnews.com/5e1fd72de08346e3ba0cecd8c9be5ac0
[132] https://fair.org/take-action/media-advisories/reagan-media-myth-and-reality/

As the nation prepares to pay tribute to former President Ronald Reagan on the one hundredth anniversary of his birth, it is amazing to consider that his success at turning the U.S. away from 1960s-style liberalism was accomplished in the face of a daily wave of news media hostility. The media's first draft of history was more myth than reality: that Reagan only brought the nation poverty, ignorance, bankruptcy, and a dangerously imbalanced foreign and defense policy.[133]

It included quotes from journalists showing their disgust for Reagan, ridiculing his economic success and agenda, and in general being the pompous jerks that they regularly are.

Some examples, all quoted from the Media Research Center:

▶ Statements people were asked to agree or disagree with in a *Washington Post*/ABC News poll released June 30, 1988:

- "President Reagan was unfair to the poor."
- "He was a rich man's president."
- "He had a negative view on women's rights."
- "He was unfair to blacks."
- "He didn't know what he was doing."
- "He was unfair to the middle class."
- "He was unfair to old people."

▶ "I think it's a dangerous failure at least in terms of programs. A mess in Central America, neglect of the poor, corruption in government.... And the worst legacy of all, the budget deficit, the impoverishment of our children." —*U.S. News & World Report* editor Roger Rosenblatt

---

[133] https://www.mrc.org/special-reports/rewriting-ronald-reagan

summarizing Reagan's record during CBS News' GOP convention coverage in 1988

▶ "I think there is a question mark on the domestic policy: I think he left an uncaring society...a government that was not as concerned." —United Press International White House reporter Helen Thomas on CBS News' *Nightwatch*, December 30, 1988

▶ "And so it goes with President Bozo...coming to the end of his eight-year reign, and reign it has been, no matter how it rained on the poor. The hell with the poor, it's their own fault; we all feel that way." —Associate Editor and longtime reporter David Nyhan in a *Boston Globe* column, December 28, 1988

▶ "Analysts will also recognize that Ronald Reagan presided over a meltdown of the federal government during the last eight years. Fundamental management was abandoned in favor of rhetoric and imagery. A cynical disregard for the art of government led to wide-scale abuse.... Only now are we coming to realize the cost of Mr. Reagan's laissez-faire: the crisis in the savings and loan industry, the scandal in the Department of Housing and Urban Development, the deterioration of the nation's nuclear weapons facilities, the dangerous state of the air traffic control system—not to mention the staggering deficit." —CBS reporter Terence Smith in a *New York Times* op-ed piece, November 5, 1989

▶ "In the 1980s the minimum wage has really lived up to its name. Since it was last raised to $3.35 an hour in 1981, inflation has eroded its purchasing power by 27 percent. Meanwhile, the Reagan era became famous for skyrocketing maximum wages as greed became fashionable throughout the land." —Associate Editor Richard Lacayo, *Time*, November 13, 1989

▶ From an exchange on PBS' *Bill Moyers: The Public Mind*, November 22, 1989:

■ Bill Moyers: "When it comes to visuals, do you miss Ronald Reagan?"

■ Lesley Stahl: "Well, I guess as a television reporter, yes, but as an American citizen, no."

▶ "The decade had its highs (Gorbachev, Bird)...and the decade had its lows (Reagan, AIDS)" —*Boston Globe* headline over two pages of 1980s reviews, December 28, 1989

▶ "By 'selling the sizzle' of Reagan, as his aide Michael Deaver put it, the administration spun the nation out of its torpor with such fantasies as supply-side economics, the nuclear weapons 'window of vulnerability,' and the Strategic Defense Initiative." —Senior Editor Harrison Rainie, *U.S. News & World Report*, December 25, 1989/January 1, 1990

▶ "It will take one hundred years to get the government back into place after Reagan. He hurt people: the disabled, women, nursing mothers, the homeless." —White House reporter Sarah McClendon, *USA Today*, February 16, 1990

▶ "The missteps, poor efforts, and setbacks brought on by the Reagan years have made this a more sober Earth Day. The task seems larger now." —*Today* cohost Bryant Gumbel, April 20, 1990

reporting—that's a negative advertising campaign in action.

If you consider the evening newscasts a reliable gauge of the liberal media at large (cable news, big newspapers, etc.), it means Biden has enjoyed an army of so-called journalists conducting a massive negative information campaign against his opponent, while he is sheltered from any scrutiny. Controversies from the spring, such as allegations from former staffer Tara Reade that he sexually assaulted her in the 1990s, completely disappeared from his evening news coverage in June and July.

Biden's various policy proposals—which by his own admission would take his administration farther to the left than the very liberal Obama administration—received a meager five minutes, twenty-two seconds of airtime, not one second of which included any critical analysis from any journalist.[137]

The Reagan presidency is over, of course, but as I write this book, President Trump has released his 2020 campaign agenda. A good way to judge a man is by the agenda he lays out. Let's take a look, before moving on to the last chapter, at Trump's Swamp-busting, in-your-face, freedom-loving agenda. The following is taken directly from his campaign website,[138] and opens up with a bold agenda and vision that Reagan would be proud of.

Building on the incredible achievements of President Donald J. Trump's first term in office, the President's re-election

---

137 https://www.newsbusters.org/blogs/nb/rich-noyes/2020/08/17/study-150-times-more-negative-news-trump-biden

138 https://www.donaldjtrump.com/media/trump-campaign-announces-president-trumps-2nd-term-agenda-fighting-for-you

campaign today released a set of core priorities for a second term under the banner of "Fighting for You!" President Trump's boundless optimism and certainty in America's greatness is reflected in his second-term goals and stands in stark contrast to the gloomy vision of America projected by Joe Biden and Democrats.

The key points support Trump's role as a freedom love and a patriot:

JOBS

- ▶ Create 10 Million New Jobs in 10 Months
- ▶ Create 1 Million New Small Businesses
- ▶ Cut Taxes to Boost Take-Home Pay and Keep Jobs in America
- ▶ Enact Fair Trade Deals that Protect American Jobs
- ▶ "Made in America" Tax Credits
- ▶ Expand Opportunity Zones
- ▶ Continue Deregulatory Agenda for Energy Independence

ERADICATE COVID-19

- ▶ Develop a Vaccine by The End Of 2020
- ▶ Return to Normal in 2021
- ▶ Make All Critical Medicines and Supplies for Healthcare Workers in The United States
- ▶ Refill Stockpiles and Prepare for Future Pandemics

END OUR RELIANCE ON CHINA

- ▶ Bring Back 1 Million Manufacturing Jobs from China

- Tax Credits for Companies that Bring Back Jobs from China
- Allow 100% Expensing Deductions for Essential Industries like Pharmaceuticals and Robotics who Bring Back their Manufacturing to the United States
- No Federal Contracts for Companies who Outsource to China
- Hold China Fully Accountable for Allowing the Virus to Spread around the World

HEALTHCARE

- Cut Prescription Drug Prices
- Put Patients and Doctors Back in Charge of our Healthcare System
- Lower Healthcare Insurance Premiums
- End Surprise Billing
- Cover All Pre-Existing Conditions
- Protect Social Security and Medicare
- Protect Our Veterans and Provide World-Class Healthcare and Services

EDUCATION

- Provide School Choice to Every Child in America
- Teach American Exceptionalism

DRAIN THE SWAMP

- Pass Congressional Term Limits
- End Bureaucratic Government Bullying of U.S. Citizens and Small Businesses

- ▶ Expose Washington's Money Trail and Delegate Powers Back to People and States
- ▶ Drain the Globalist Swamp by Taking on International Organizations That Hurt American Citizens

DEFEND OUR POLICE

- ▶ Fully Fund and Hire More Police and Law Enforcement Officers
- ▶ Increase Criminal Penalties for Assaults on Law Enforcement Officers
- ▶ Prosecute Drive-By Shootings as Acts of Domestic Terrorism
- ▶ Bring Violent Extremist Groups Like ANTIFA to Justice
- ▶ End Cashless Bail and Keep Dangerous Criminals Locked Up until Trial

END ILLEGAL IMMIGRATION AND PROTECT AMERICAN WORKERS

- ▶ Block Illegal Immigrants from Becoming Eligible for Taxpayer-Funded Welfare, Healthcare, and Free College Tuition
- ▶ Mandatory Deportation for Non-Citizen Gang Members
- ▶ Dismantle Human Trafficking Networks
- ▶ End Sanctuary Cities to Restore our Neighborhoods and Protect our Families
- ▶ Prohibit American Companies from Replacing United States Citizens with Lower-Cost Foreign Workers

immutable characteristics. The American way of life is being dismantled by a group of bitter, deceitful, vengeful, activists who have never built anything in their lives. They have us locking up pastors while releasing violent criminals from prison....

We will be a country that makes it easier to have many children, live quiet and peaceable lives, and worship your God without a tyrant getting in the way. We will be a country that has its best one hundred years ahead. We will build a future where America remains the greatest country ever to exist in the history of the world. All of that is within our grasp if we secure four more years for the defender of Western civilization, our champion, my friend, the forty-fifth president of the United States, President Donald J. Trump.[139135]

The media are relentlessly anti-Trump and anti-conservative. They regularly seek to undermine freedom, liberty, and American democracy. Another huge threat to our liberty comes from the foreign policy establishment. In that arena, Reagan and Trump also became unlikely heroes, as we shall see in the next chapter.

CHAPTER 5

FOREIGN POLICY WINS

"We understand that both of our countries are stronger when we join forces in matters of international commerce. Having more jobs and trade right here in North America is better for both the United States and is also much better for Canada. We should coordinate closely—and we will coordinate closely—to protect jobs in our hemisphere and keep wealth on our continent, and to keep everyone safe."

—President Donald Trump at a joint press conference with Canadian prime minister Justin Trudeau, 2017[140]

"Common sense also told us that to preserve the peace, we'd have to become strong again after years of weakness and confusion. So, we rebuilt our defenses, and this New Year we toasted the new peacefulness around the globe. Not only have the superpowers actually begun to reduce their stockpiles of nuclear weapons—and hope for even more progress is bright—but the regional conflicts that rack the

---

140   https://www.whitehouse.gov/briefings-statements/remarks-president-trump-prime-minister-trudeau-canada-joint-press-conference/

globe are also beginning to cease. The Persian Gulf is no longer a war zone. The Soviets are leaving Afghanistan. The Vietnamese are preparing to pull out of Cambodia, and an American-mediated accord will soon send fifty thousand Cuban troops home from Angola."

—President Ronald Reagan in his
second farewell address, 1989[141]

"Libya was cooperating. Egypt was peaceful. Iraq was seeing a reduction in violence. Iran was being choked by sanctions. Syria was under control. After four years of Hillary Clinton, what do we have? ISIS has spread across the region, and the world. Libya is in ruins, and our Ambassador and his staff were left helpless to die at the hands of savage killers. Egypt was turned over to the radical Muslim brotherhood, forcing the military to retake control. Iraq is in chaos. Iran is on the path to nuclear weapons."

—candidate Donald Trump in his Republican National Convention speech, 2016[142]

"President Trump is the first president since Reagan not to start a new war. Biden has foolishly cheered decades of war without winning, without end. President Trump knows we are strongest when we fight hardest, not in distant deserts, but for our fellow Americans."

—Representative Matt Gaetz (Republican from Florida) in his Republican National Convention speech, 2020[143]

---

[141] https://millercenter.org/the-presidency/presidential-speeches/january-11-1989-farewell-address

[142] https://www.politico.com/story/2016/07/full-transcript-donald-trump-nomination-acceptance-speech-at-rnc-225974

[143] https://www.rev.com/blog/transcripts/2020-republican-national-convention-rnc-night-1-transcript

And repeating from the previous chapter, Trump's 2020 agenda for foreign policy:

AMERICA FIRST FOREIGN POLICY

▶ *Stop Endless Wars and Bring Our Troops Home*
▶ *Get Allies to Pay their Fair Share*
▶ *Maintain and Expand America's Unrivaled Military Strength*
▶ *Wipe Out Global Terrorists Who Threaten to Harm Americans*
▶ *Build a Great Cybersecurity Defense System and Missile Defense System*

President Trump and President Reagan took on the foreign policy establishment in their own party, including neoconservatives. For Trump that presently includes Never Trumpers like Bill Kristol, who are always advocating for needless wars and for sending other people's kids overseas to satiate their own lust for war. For example, Kristol at one time advocated for a regime change in Iran simply because, I assume, he wants to continue to pump up the military-industrial complex.[144]

And of course the Democratic Party, despite every four years pretending to like peace, actually supports war and the military-industrial complex. Democrats preferred to have a president and secretary of state who could not be woken from their slumber to save brave U.S. foreign officers who were in the midst of a fire that they themselves created. I am, of course, referring to the way that Barack Obama and Hillary Clinton

---

[144]   https://www.npr.org/2011/12/13/143633939/weekly-standard-is-irans-clock-ticking

teamed up to bring down Libya and allowed the embassy to burn.

Political science professor Dominic Tierney wrote of the aftermath in *The Atlantic*:

> In Afghanistan, Iraq, and Libya, Washington toppled regimes and then failed to plan for a new government or construct effective local forces—with the net result being over seven thousand dead U.S. soldiers, tens of thousands of injured troops, trillions of dollars expended, untold thousands of civilian fatalities, and three Islamic countries in various states of disorder. We might be able to explain a one-off failure in terms of allies screwing up. But three times in a decade suggests a deeper pattern in the American way of war....
>
> In war, there are two good options for the United States. The first is regime change with a viable plan to win the peace. The second option is not to go to war at all. There is no point in toppling a tyrant if the result is anarchy.[145]

The foreign policy Swamp monsters are like no other. The deep state radicals use the State Department to undermine U.S. interests, to screw over American workers, and to promote values that are antithetical to what most Americans want. This includes using our federal taxpayer dollars to attack valuable energy interests and to coerce women around the world into having abortions as part of the never-ending drive by hardcore leftists to promote a global eugenics mission.

---

[145] https://www.theatlantic.com/international/archive/2016/04/obamas-worst-mistake-libya/478461/

If I had to guess—and I'm taking hyperbolic liberties here—I would say that about 15 percent of the State Department are hardworking people who want to help people around the world, want to keep America safe, and want to ensure that American interests are protected. The other 85 percent *love* power, and I mean truly *love* power. They love the idea of taking their graduate degree in women and gender studies from Oberlin and helping funnel money to international abortion vendors. They use their doctoral dissertation on "queerness implicit in poststructural modernism" to foist a homosexual agenda on religious, conservative countries around the world. From their government-issued laptop and phone, they can return to the feeling of power they once had as the student body president at their private high school in New York.

What these people do is drive up and down I-95 in Virginia or I-495 and plot ways to undermine American freedom and liberty. Perhaps they use their influence to direct taxpayer dollars to radical leftist groups or racist groups. Or they figure out ways to support radical Islamic groups while trying to denigrate Christians.

President Trump has taken on the deep-state Swamp and, at a minimum, helped expose and bring to light the misdeeds of the State Department. Many people think of the State Department as an agency that grants passports or runs embassies around the world; in reality, the State Department is a Swamp monster that wastes our money on causes that most people do not support.

Consider what journalist James O'Keefe uncovered in 2018 at the State Department. The agency's employees, as sworn members of the deep state, were plotting to take down Trump.

The *Washington Times* reported:

Project Veritas has caught a State Department bureaucrat on hidden camera proclaiming he is part of the anti-Trump opposition and his job is to "resist everything" at "every level."

> Conservative activist and Veritas chief James O'Keefe released the video on Tuesday. He said it kicks off what he promises is wide exposure of the so-called "deep state" actively working to defeat President Trump from within via media leaks and policy sabotage.
>
> "What you are about to see is the hidden face of the resistance inside the executive branch of our government," Mr. O'Keefe said. Of course, as the State Department employee notes, he can do whatever he wants because it's impossible to fire federal employees.[146]

Sebastian Gorka, a former adviser to President Trump, has laid out the threats to the nation from the deep state as well.

In February 2020, he wrote about the deep state in a column for the *Epoch Times*. Gorka said he had attended meetings with high-ranking officials, and they rarely talked about how their proposed plans fit in with the president's agenda:

At the highest national security policymaking level of the nation, outside of the Oval Office, I saw the same behavior. However long the meeting, one hour or longer, whoever was in the room and on the secure outstation screens—the CIA, DIA, Joint Chiefs, NSA, etc.—no one in the room or on the net would mention the commander-in-chief's name, or what the president had said with regard to the specific issue we were there

---

[146] https://www.washingtontimes.com/news/2018/sep/18/stuart-karaffa-state-department-bureaucrat-caught-/

to grapple with.... The unelected bureaucrats couldn't care less that sixty-three million Americans had chosen a new president and a new path for America—they were America's collective master.[147]

Gorka says his preferred personnel for his projects were delayed, the deep state doing what it could to slow Trump's agenda. He said the FBI views Trump as the enemy, and agents slow-walk his appointees through background checks and security clearance procedures.

Gorka concluded:

> It's remarkable that President Trump has survived so far against a federal bureaucracy so riven through with seditious and criminal actors, let alone achieved so much in just three and a half years.
>
> If he survives the continued machinations of the deep state and its collaborators in the mainstream media and is, God willing, reelected, his biggest challenge will not be natural or manmade biological agents from abroad. It will be the enemy that lies within the halls of his own government.

President Trump needs to grab the deep state by the throat right now. Before it's too late.

Praise for Trump's Foreign Policy

Prime Minister of Israel Benjamin Netanyahu in 2017:

---

[147] https://www.theepochtimes.com/coronavirus-isnt-the-biggest-threat-we-face-by-far_3253416.html

In over 30 years in my experience with the UN, I never heard a bolder or more courageous speech. President Trump spoke the truth about the great dangers facing our world and issued a powerful call to confront them in order to ensure the future of humanity.[148]

Republican Jewish Coalition director Matt Brooks praising Trump's strong words in support of Israel:

Today's speech at the UN was an historic moment for President Trump and the American people. The president's speech set out a clear, unambiguous vision that America will always work in the best interests of its citizens and will always work with responsible countries around the globe to keep the world safe and secure. There is no greater example of this vision than President Trump's commitments, reemphasized today, to confront the reckless nuclear aspirations of Iran and North Korea, to oppose the brutal regime of Syria, and to combat radical Islamic terrorism at home and abroad. The president was strong in his condemnation of Iran as a corrupt dictatorship, economically depleted, a destabilizing force in the Middle East, and a chief exporter of violence and terror. And, as he has many times before, the president called the Iran nuclear deal a terribly flawed and ineffective agreement. Today's speech was a strong affirmation of American leadership on the world stage, something that has been missing during the last eight years. The RJC applauds President Trump.

---

[148] https://www.whitehouse.gov/briefings-statements/praise-president-donald-j-trumps-address-un-general-assembly/

Senator Tom Cotton (Republican from Arkansas), commenting on the swift and decisive actions taken by Trump regarding the Iran deal:

> Lawmakers need to do now what we couldn't do two years ago: unite around an Iran strategy that truly stops Iran's nuclear weapons program and empowers the United States and our allies to combat the full spectrum of Iran's imperial aggression. The legislation Senator Corker and I have been working on with the administration will address the major flaws in the original Iran deal: the sunset clauses, the weak inspections regime, and the failure to restrict Iran's development of advanced centrifuges. And it will create time and leverage for firm diplomacy—together with our allies—to work and neutralize the threat of a nuclear Iran permanently.[149]

Senator Roger Wicker (Republican from Mississippi):

> I continue to believe that the pact with Iran, negotiated by the Obama administration, is a terrible deal for America and our allies. Iran is still the leading state sponsor of terrorism, and its illegal ballistic missile program is advancing. By his actions today, President Trump is giving us the opportunity to strengthen our hand to hold Tehran accountable. Decertification does not end U.S. participation in the agreement, but it does represent the first step toward negotiating a better deal.[150]

---

[149] https://www.whitehouse.gov/briefings-statements/praise-president-donald-j-trumps-new-strategy-iran/

[150] https://www.whitehouse.gov/briefings-statements/praise-president-donald-j-trumps-new-strategy-iran/

Speaking of wasteful taxpayer-funded institutions, President Trump also took on the foreign policy Establishment by criticizing NATO and exposing the fraud that is NATO (as well as defunding the World Health Organization—more on that later!).

As a presidential candidate, Trump said:

> I think NATO is obsolete. NATO was done at a time you had the Soviet Union, which was obviously larger—much larger than Russia is today. I'm not saying Russia is not a threat.
>
> But we have other threats. We have the threat of terrorism. And NATO doesn't discuss terrorism. NATO's not meant for terrorism. NATO doesn't have the right countries in it for terrorism.
>
> And what I'm saying is that we pay, number one, a totally disproportionate share of NATO. We're spending—the biggest alliance share is paid for by us, disproportionate to other countries.
>
> And if you look at the Ukraine, we're the ones always fighting on the Ukraine. I never hear any other countries even mentioned, and we're fighting constantly. We're talking about Ukraine, 'Get out, do this, do that.'"[151]

Foreign policy leaders have thanked Trump for taking on NATO.

President Trump also made a tremendous move by withdrawing from the disgraced Chinese Communist Party-connected World Health Organization after it botched the

---

[151] https://www.realclearpolitics.com/video/2016/03/27/trump_europe_is_not_safe_lots_of_the_free_world_has_become_weak.html

handling of the coronavirus. The decision was hailed for a variety of medical, foreign policy, and life-related reasons.

The pro-life group Students for Life of America criticized the World Health Organization and thanked Trump for his decision:

The calculated attempt to waste taxpayer resources on abortions at this critical moment in attempting to slow and stop the coronavirus crisis shows just how little the World Health Organization is focused on the real problem. Abortion is not a cure for pregnancy or the coronavirus. Rather than directing their efforts at problem solving, the WHO has taken a side job as an abortion lobbyist. On their website they proudly report that one in four pregnancies end in abortion worldwide. The WHO should focus their efforts on protecting the lives of people, born and preborn, rather than pressuring governments to find abortion "essential."[152]

The libertarian *Reason* magazine also praised Trump's decision, saying the U.S. had little to fear from the decision:

The WHO's record on tackling COVID-19 has been a catalog of errors. Even supporters of the organization acknowledge the institution needs fundamental reform. As it stands, the WHO lacks accountability and has not represented good value for the money spent by U.S. taxpayers....

Instead of preparing the world for a disastrous pandemic, the WHO has busied itself with counterproductive and unscientific campaigns against vaping and urging governments to regulate people's lifestyle choices.

---

[152] https://studentsforlife.org/2020/04/15/president-trump-defunds-pro-abortion-world-health-organization/

Withdrawing support for the WHO is not synonymous with withdrawing support for world health. The U.S. government can and will continue to engage with countries around the world to limit the damage from COVID-19. The private and nonprofit sectors will continue to advance public health goals.[153]

In fact, before Trump championed the idea, the Associated Press admitted in 2017 that the WHO lacked accountability for their spending. It found:

[T]he U.N. health agency routinely has spent about $200 million a year on travel expenses, more than what it doles out to fight some of the biggest problems in public health, including AIDS, tuberculosis and malaria combined.

Last year, WHO spent about $71 million on AIDS and hepatitis. It devoted $61 million to malaria. To slow the spread of tuberculosis, WHO invested $59 million. Still, some health programs do get exceptional funding—the agency spends about $450 million trying to wipe out polio every year.[154]

But only Trump actually took the bold step of defunding the World Health Organization.

Reagan took similarly bold leadership steps in foreign policy by staring down the Soviet Union, even traveling to Germany to boldly tell the Kremlin to tear down the Berlin Wall dividing East and West Germany. The mainstream media and the

---

[153] https://reason.org/commentary/the-us-has-little-to-fear-from-cutting-off-the-unaccountable-world-health-organizations-funding/

[154] https://apnews.com/article/1cf4791dc5c14b9299e0f532c75f63b2

foreign policy elites hated the idea; they derided it and thought it was dangerous.

Even his own staffers feared the idea. The news website VOA reported, "On 12 June, 1987, when U.S. president Ronald Reagan called on Soviet leader Mikhail Gorbachev to tear down the Berlin Wall, some of his staffers thought Mr. Reagan's words were too hostile, and could harm U.S.-Soviet relations."[155]

But Reagan biographer Lou Cannon explained why Reagan moved forward with his plans to call for the tearing down of the wall. "He had toured the wall that morning, and if you tour that wall, it's very emotional because you saw this graffitti [sic] and these tributes to people who had died crossing the wall," he told VOA.

The Reagan Foundation explained Reagan's vision:

> He believed fervently in the greatness and goodness of America, and knew that American strength was central to world peace. One of his first priorities as president was taking a demoralized and underfunded U.S. military and giving it the support and resources it needed to keep America safe and to be a force for peace around the globe. Nothing made him prouder than to be commander in chief. You could see in his face how much it meant to receive— and return—a salute. He felt a special bond with the men and women in uniform, especially the young people from the small towns across America. That they were willing to risk their lives for their country never ceased to amaze and humble President Reagan. He took no responsibility more seriously than to keep them out of harm's way. But

---

[155] https://www.voanews.com/archive/reagan-biographer-remembers-controversy-surrounding-berlin-wall-speech

he made a commitment to them that if it ever became necessary to send them into battle, he would make sure they had what they needed to get the job done. By the time President Reagan left office, the U.S. military budget had increased 43 percent over the total expenditure during the height of the Vietnam War. Troop levels increased, there were significantly more weapons and equipment, and the country's intelligence program was vastly improved.[156]

Furthermore, while the Foggy Bottom Establishment derided Reagan's approach to the Soviet Union, historical analysis of his decisions proves that he was indeed correct.

President Reagan, like Trump, worked to avoid needless, endless wars (though of course he could not fully avoid military conflict). He instead pursued an aggressive strategy to build up our military in the same way Trump later did. Through this, we achieved peace through strength.

The Heritage Foundation explained how Reagan implemented "Peace through Strength" to keep our country safe and strong.

The conservative organization, in its description of a panel discussion it was hosting, said:

> President Reagan's often mocked strategy of "peace through strength" won the Cold War. Critical to that success were his nuclear deterrent polices. By both modernizing our strategic nuclear deterrence while also initiating what would become a nearly 90 percent reduction in American

---

[156]   https://www.reaganfoundation.org/ronald-reagan/the-presidency/foreign-policy/

and Soviet (now Russian) deployed strategic nuclear warheads—he changed the strategic nuclear landscape.[157]

Doug Bandow, a former assistant to President Reagan, wrote this of Reagan's legacy:

> Ronald Reagan's mantra was "peace through strength." Peace was the end, strength the means. He focused on the Soviet Union and its advanced outposts, especially in the Western Hemisphere.
>
> Restraining the hegemonic threat posed by an aggressive, ideological Soviet Union led to Reagan's tough policy. Still, Reagan avoided military confrontation with Moscow. Indeed, he routinely employed what neocons today deride as "appeasement."
>
> For instance, Reagan dropped the Carter grain embargo against Moscow. Reagan said he desired to encourage "meaningful and constructive dialogue."
>
> Lech Walesa and the Solidarity movement were a global inspiration but the Polish military, fearing Soviet intervention, imposed martial law in 1981. No American bombers flew, no invasion threatened, no soldiers marched. Reagan waited for the Evil Empire to further deteriorate from within.
>
> However, Reagan wanted to negotiate—from a position of strength, but he still wanted to negotiate."[158]

Reagan, like Trump, was not afraid to talk straight to the global enemies of freedom, such as the United Nations. In 1987,

---

[157] https://www.heritage.org/missile-defense/event/reagans-peace-through-strength-cold-war-strategy-integrating-defense-nuclear

[158] https://www.cato.org/blog/ronald-reagan-peace-through-strength-did-not-mean-war-any-price

Reagan went to the UN and laid out clearly what needed to be fixed. He used his skills as a great communicator to be an unlikely hero to Americans who were suspicious of the foreign policy Establishment. Reagan boldly took his message of free markets and economic liberty and democracy to the despots and dictators that run the United Nations:

> But true statesmanship requires not merely skill but something greater, something we call vision—a grasp of the present and of the possibilities of the future. I've come here today to map out for you my own vision of the world's future, one, I believe, that in its essential elements is shared by all Americans. And I hope those who see things differently will not mind if I say that we in the United States believe that the place to look first for shape of the future is not in continental masses and sea lanes, although geography is, obviously, of great importance. Neither is it in national reserves of blood and iron or, on the other hand, of money and industrial capacity, although military and economic strength are also, of course, crucial. We begin with something that is far simpler and yet far more profound: the human heart....
>
> In India and China, freer markets for farmers have led to an explosion in production. In Africa, governments are rethinking their policies, and where they are allowing greater economic freedom to farmers, crop production has improved. Meanwhile, in the newly industrialized countries of the Pacific rim, free markets in services and manufacturing as well as agriculture have led to a soaring of growth and standards of living. The ASEAN nations, Japan, Korea, and Taiwan, have created the true economic miracle of the last two decades, and in each of them, much

of the magic came from ordinary people who succeeded as entrepreneurs.

In Latin America, this same lesson of free markets, greater opportunity, and growth is being studied and acted on. President Sarney of Brazil spoke for many others when he said that "private initiative is the engine of economic development. In Brazil we have learned that every time the state's penetration in the economy increases, our liberty decreases." Yes, policies that release to flight ordinary people's dreams are spreading around the world. From Colombia to Turkey to Indonesia, governments are cutting taxes, reviewing their regulations, and opening opportunities for initiative....

Those who advocate statist solutions to development should take note: the free market is the other path to development and the one true path. And unlike many other paths, it leads somewhere. It works. So, this is where I believe we can find the map to the world's future: in the hearts of ordinary people, in their hopes for themselves and their children, in their prayers as they lay themselves and their families to rest each night. These simple people are the giants of the earth, the true builders of the world and shapers of the centuries to come. And if indeed they triumph, as I believe they will, we will at last know a world of peace and freedom, opportunity and hope, and, yes, of democracy—a world in which the spirit of mankind at last conquers the old, familiar enemies of famine, disease, tyranny, and war.

This is my vision—America's vision. I recognize that some governments represented in this hall have other ideas. Some do not believe in democracy or in political, economic, or religious freedom. Some believe in dictatorship, whether by one man, one party, one class, one race, or one vanguard. To those governments I would only say that the price of oppression is clear. Your economies will fall farther and farther behind. Your people will become more restless. Isn't it better to listen to the people's hopes now rather than their curses later?[159]

Another way that globalists tried to push their radical agenda was through the Paris Accord, which President Obama signed us on to and President Trump correctly pulled us out of.

Here are some criticisms of the Paris Accord, which basically surrendered our economy to globalist elites in Europe. They come courtesy of the Competitive Enterprise Institute:

> In America's constitutional system, treaties must obtain the advice and consent of the Senate before the United States may lawfully join them. President Obama deemed the Paris Agreement to not be a treaty in order to evade constitutional review, which the Agreement almost certainly would not have survived....
>
> The United States cannot comply with the Paris Agreement and pursue a pro-growth energy agenda. Affordable, plentiful, reliable energy is the lifeblood of modern economic life. Yet, the Paris Agreement's central goal is to make fossil fuels, America's most plentiful and affordable energy source, more expensive across the board. Implementing the agreement's progressively more restrictive five-year emission-reduction pledges—called Nationally Determined Contributions (NDCs)—would destroy U.S. manufacturing's energy price edge....

---

[159] https://www.reaganlibrary.gov/research/speeches/092187b

Withdrawing from the Paris Agreement is a humanitarian imperative. The Agreement will produce no detectable climate benefits. Instead, it will divert trillions of dollars from productive investments that would advance global welfare to political uses.[160]

Another respected think tank, the American Enterprise Institute, praised Trump for withdrawing from the globalist Paris Accord. Economist and former intelligence staffer Ben Zycher concluded:

Because the central ideological goal of the climate industry is an elimination of fossil fuels, the planet will never be saved and the goalposts will be moved continually. Accordingly, the Paris agreement is silly and destructive as a strategy to engender environmental improvement, but it works beautifully as a mechanism to transform the climate industry into a perpetual motion machine. President Trump is wise to reject it.[161]

---

161 https://www.aei.org/profile/benjamin-zycher/

CHAPTER 6

GREATNESS

"I have been involved in three really disruptive experiences in my career. The first was in the late seventies, early eighties with Ronald Reagan, who just shook everything up. There were periods where people thought that he was a cowboy from out West and didn't know what he was doing. [Reagan] took a foreign policy that was failing, and nine years later, the Soviet Union disappeared—that was disruption....I would have to say, in all honesty, Trump is a much bigger disruptor than I was....I think the only two comparable disruptors were Andrew Jackson, who in personality was much more like Trump, and Abraham Lincoln, who by circumstance couldn't avoid it. He had to preside over and win a civil war.... I think that if you look at the two hundred judges he's gotten approved, if you look at the regulations he's repealed, if you look at the power of the ideas he's been pushing, he will go down in history as one of the most disruptive figures ever to lead the United States."

—former speaker of the house
Newt Gingrich[162]

Presidents Reagan and Trump, as you no doubt know by now, are similar in many ways. To recap, they inspired new hope in people who had lost hope. They helped culture warriors win important victories in the areas of free speech, law and order, abortion, and transgenderism. Furthermore, they shook up the Foggy Bottom foreign policy Establishment by putting pressure on international institutions.

The D.C. Swamp monsters opposed them at all turns, trying to undermine Reagan and Trump so they could stay in power. Both presidents faced down similar enemies: big banks. The Establishment. Globalists. Their own party, and of course the Democratic Party too.

Donald Trump Jr. spoke of Trump's vision at the 2020 Republican National Convention:

Imagine a world where the evils of communism and radical Islamic terrorism are not given a chance to spread, where heroes are celebrated and the good guys win. You can have it. That is the life, that is the country, that is the world that Donald Trump and the Republican Party are after. And yes, you can have it because unlike Joe Biden and the radical-left Democrats, our party is open to everyone. It starts by rejecting radicals who want to drag us into the dark and embracing the man who represents a bright and beautiful future for all.[163]

Reagan and Trump both displayed strong decision-making skills, the ability to communicate well, and the ability to trust their instincts, not the *New York Times* editorial board.

---

[163]   https://www.rev.com/transcript-editor/shared/BqMflekGOaYROC-qtVwZprRgQUPjhUKDP1_bBMz0z_XfU7UHdeL5VTx8lo7vNbO-JvNFeknzqJZTr4Alwt-hFs2-3uSQ?loadFrom=PastedDeeplink&ts=3759.17

They listened to the American people, Middle America, common-sense Americans. They didn't look to globalist banks or high-paid political consultants to tell them what to do.

Trump also took on NATO, forcing lazy countries to finally pitch in their fair share for being protected by our brave men and women in uniform. These brave men and women sacrifice a normal life and one of safety in order to defend our so-called allies. The best these allies can do is pay their fair share.

As a naturalized citizen of the United States—which means I did it the right way, through *legal* means, I look up to both President Reagan and President Trump. Reagan's softer approach and folksy charm helped him win over allies and cast himself as a likable guy. President Trump is a likable guy too, but he's more like the guy you want on your side during a fight. He can be tough, he can be rough, but he's the one you want standing in front of you during a fight. He will talk tough on China, with Nancy Pelosi, and with the thugs and criminals who seek to undermine the great American system of law and order. We need people like President Reagan and President Trump.

As Reagan said in 1967:

> Without respect for the law, the best laws cannot be effective. Without respect for law enforcement, laws cannot be carried out. We must have respect, not only for the law but also for the many who dedicate their lives to the protection of society through enforcement of the law.[164]

And as Trump said in 2020:

---

[164]   https://www.reaganlibrary.gov/research/speeches/01161967a

[W]e cannot allow the righteous prize and peaceful protesters to be drowned out by an angry mob. The biggest victims of the rioting are peace-loving citizens in our poorest communities, and as their President, I will fight to keep them safe. I will fight to protect you. I am your president of law and order and an ally of all peaceful protesters.

We have one, beautiful law. And once that is restored and fully restored, we will help you, we will help your business, and we will help your family. America is founded on the rule of law. It is the foundation of our prosperity, our freedom, and our very way of life, but where there is no law, there is no opportunity. Where there is no justice, there is no liberty; where there is no safety, there is no future. We must never give in to anger or hatred. If malice or violence reigns, then none of us is free. I take these actions today with firm resolve and with a true and passionate love for our country. By far our greatest days lie ahead.[165]

I and those like me felt like President Trump was finally someone saying *no* to the leftist Establishment, the mainstream media. He was saying no to the fake-news outlet CNN, to the enemies of the people, to the race hustlers of the U.S., and to our so-called allies in NATO that rip us off on defense funding and our so-called allies to the north and south that robbed America of good middle-class jobs through NAFTA. Trump was finally someone who stood up for blue-collar voters, for Christians, for small-business owners, for gun owners.

Trump said it incredibly well and in a genius manner when he condemned violent protests in the summer of 2020

---

[165] https://www.cnn.com/2020/06/01/politics/read-trumps-rose-garden-remarks/index.html

stemming from the death of George Floyd at the hands of Minneapolis police officers. He correctly condemned the killing of Floyd and praised *peaceful* protests but laid down the law:

> [O]ur nation has been gripped by professional anarchists, violent mobs, or arsonists, looters, criminals, rider rioters, Antifa, and others. A number of state and local governors have failed to take necessary action to safeguard their residence. Innocent people have been savagely beaten, like the young man in Dallas, Texas, who was left dying on the street. Or the woman in upstate New York, viciously attacked by dangerous thugs. Small-business owners have seen their dreams utterly destroyed. New York's finest have been hit in the face with bricks. Brave nurses who have battled the virus are afraid to leave their homes. A police precinct has been overrun here in the nation's capital; the Lincoln Memorial and the World War II memorial have been vandalized. One of our most historic churches was set ablaze. A federal officer in California, an African American enforcement hero, was shot and killed.
>
> These are not acts of peaceful protest. These are acts of domestic terror. The destruction of innocent life and the spilling of innocent blood is [an] offense to humanity and a crime against god. America needs creation, not destruction. Cooperation, not contempt. Security, not anarchy. Healing the hatred, justice, not chaos. This is our mission, and we will succeed one hundred percent. We will succeed. Our country always wins. That is why I am taking immediate presidential action to stop the violence and restore security and safety in America. I am immobilizing all federal resources, civilian and military, to stop the rioting and looting, to end the destruction and arson, and

to protect the rights of law-abiding Americans, including your Second Amendment rights. Therefore, the following measures are going into effect immediately.[166]

Reagan said in October 1988, a few weeks before his vice president, George H. W. Bush, faced reelection as president:

No matter how you look at it, the last time they were in office, the liberals clobbered the American middle class— and we stopped them. Some are calling this last-ditch opposition campaign an attempt at "class warfare." So, what's new? Our liberal friends have been at war with America's middle class for years. Now they want you to turn the other cheek—but will they just take that as an opportunity to really let you have it? Main Street America is in better shape today than it's ever been. Why would we ever want to put it back in the hands of those who almost turned out its lights?[167]

And it's true. Most liberal elites, those in power, wake up every day seeking to undermine the foundations of the country. They want to take away our jobs, our guns, and our religion.

In his first inaugural address, Trump stated:

Millions of our fellow citizens are watching us now, gathered in this great chamber, hoping that we will govern not as two parties but as one nation.

The agenda I will lay out this evening is not a Republican agenda or a Democrat agenda. It's the agenda of the American people.

---

[166] https://www.whitehouse.gov/briefings-statements/statement-by-the-president-39/

[167] https://www.reaganlibrary.gov/research/speeches/102288a

Many of us have campaigned on the same core promises: to defend American jobs and demand fair trade for
American workers; to rebuild and revitalize our nation's
infrastructure; to reduce the price of healthcare and
prescription drugs; to create an immigration system that is
safe, lawful, modern, and secure; and to pursue a foreign
policy that puts America's interests first."[168]

We need both parties to put Americans first. We have too
many elites in power who hate guns. They hate oil. They hate
freedom. Only a love of country—the type of love that Trump
and Reagan, our unlikely heroes, espoused—can bring us
together as Americans.

Our country is at a crossroads. On one side, we have the
big-money interests: the globalist banks, the well-funded foundations. They give money to ANTIFA to loot and riot, they fund
leftist professors at colleges, and they fund leftist politicians like
Chuck Schumer and Nancy Pelosi. On the other side, we have
hardworking Americans who grow our food, fight our wars, and
build the things we use every day. We should always focus our
efforts on supporting *those people!*

It is a point President Reagan made so well in his 1981 inaugural address:

We hear much of special interest groups. Well, our concern
must be for a special interest group that has been too long
neglected. It knows no sectional boundaries or ethnic and
racial divisions, and it crosses political party lines. It is
made up of men and women who raise our food, patrol our

---

[168] https://www.whitehouse.gov/briefings-statements/
remarks-president-trump-state-union-address-2/

streets, man our mines and factories, teach our children, keep our homes, and heal us when we're sick—professionals, industrialists, shopkeepers, clerks, cabbies, and truckdrivers. They are, in short, "We the people," this breed called Americans. Well, this administration's objective will be a healthy, vigorous, growing economy that provides equal opportunities for all Americans with no barriers born of bigotry or discrimination. Putting America back to work means putting all Americans back to work. Ending inflation means freeing all Americans from the terror of runaway living costs. All must share in the productive work of this "new beginning," and all must share in the bounty of a revived economy. With the idealism and fair play which are the core of our system and our strength, we can have a strong and prosperous America, at peace with itself and the world.[169]

President Trump is my president. He set aside a life of working for himself as the CEO of one of the most prosperous and successful companies in the United States so that he could work for you and me. President Reagan left a successful broadcasting career so that he could right the ship and put us back on the right path. Along the way, both made their share of mistakes, but they cannot be faulted for not being doctrinaire conservatives their whole lives. What truly matters is that when our country needed them, Trump and Reagan answered the call.

For this, we should be eternally thankful and grateful. Reagan and Trump dedicated years of their lives to defending our most sacred honors and fighting for the American ideal—an America where everyone would have a chance at a good job

[169] https://www.reaganfoundation.org/media/128614/inaguration.pdf

and a good education, and the chance to build wealth and take advantage of numerous opportunities. They did it in the face of inheriting awful economies and a divided country from weak leaders like Jimmy Carter and Barack Obama, respectively.

They did it in the face of manufactured racial unrest and social worries, ginned up by the left-wing fake-news media.

When Reagan died, his longtime adversary, Soviet leader Mikhail Gorbachev, said:

> I deem Ronald Reagan a great president, with whom the Soviet leadership was able to launch a very difficult but important dialogue....
>
> Reagan was a statesman who, despite all disagreements that existed between our countries at the time, displayed foresight and determination to meet our proposals halfway and change our relations for the better, stop the nuclear race, start scrapping nuclear weapons, and arrange normal relations between our countries.[170]

He respected Reagan, although the left-wing mainstream media said that foreign leaders would not. This statement means a lot.

One day Trump's opponents will say the same thing about him.

APPENDIX

SPEECHES

President Donald Trump's State of the Union Address

January 30, 2018
Remarks as prepared for delivery.
To the Congress of the United States:

Mr. Speaker, Mr. Vice President, members of Congress, the First Lady of the United States, and my fellow Americans:

Less than one year has passed since I first stood at this podium, in this majestic chamber, to speak on behalf of the American people—and to address their concerns, their hopes, and their dreams. That night, our new administration had already taken swift action. A new tide of optimism was already sweeping across our land.

Each day since, we have gone forward with a clear vision and a righteous mission—to make America great again for all Americans.

Over the last year, we have made incredible progress and achieved extraordinary success. We have faced challenges we expected, and others we could never have imagined. We have shared in the heights of victory and the pains of hardship. We endured floods and fires and storms. But through it all, we have seen the beauty of America's soul and the steel in America's spine.

Each test has forged new American heroes to remind us who we are and show us what we can be.

We saw the volunteers of the "Cajun Navy" racing to the rescue with their fishing boats to save people in the aftermath of a devastating hurricane.

We saw strangers shielding strangers from a hail of gunfire on the Las Vegas Strip.

We heard tales of Americans like Coast Guard petty officer Ashlee Leppert, who is here tonight in the gallery with Melania. Ashlee was aboard one of the first helicopters on the scene in Houston during Hurricane Harvey. Through eighteen hours of wind and rain, Ashlee braved live power lines and deep water to help save more than forty lives. Thank you, Ashlee.

We heard about Americans like firefighter David Dahlberg. He is here with us too. David faced down walls of flame to rescue almost sixty children trapped at a California summer camp threatened by wildfires.

To everyone still recovering in Texas, Florida, Louisiana, Puerto Rico, the Virgin Islands, California, and everywhere else—we are with you, we love you, and we will pull through together.

Some trials over the past year touched this chamber very personally. With us tonight is one of the toughest people ever to serve in this House—a guy who took a bullet, almost died, and was back to work three and a half months later: the legend from Louisiana, Congressman Steve Scalise.

We are incredibly grateful for the heroic efforts of the Capitol police officers, the Alexandria police, and the doctors, nurses, and paramedics who saved his life and the lives of many others in this room.

In the aftermath of that terrible shooting, we came together, not as Republicans or Democrats, but as representatives of the people. But it is not enough to come together only in times of tragedy. Tonight, I call upon all of us to set aside our differences, to seek out common ground, and to summon the unity we need to deliver for the people we were elected to serve.

Over the last year, the world has seen what we always knew: that no people on Earth are so fearless, or daring, or determined as Americans. If there is a mountain, we climb it. If there is a frontier, we cross it. If there is a challenge, we tame it. If there is an opportunity, we seize it.

So let us begin tonight by recognizing that the state of our union is strong because our people are strong.

And together, we are building a safe, strong, and proud America.

Since the election, we have created 2.4 million new jobs, including two hundred thousand new jobs in manufacturing alone. After years of wage stagnation, we are finally seeing rising wages.

Unemployment claims have hit a forty-five-year low. African American unemployment stands at the lowest rate ever recorded, and Hispanic American unemployment has also reached the lowest levels in history.

Small-business confidence is at an all-time high. The stock market has smashed one record after another, gaining eight trillion dollars in value. That is great news for Americans' 401(k), retirement, pension, and college savings accounts.

And just as I promised the American people from this podium eleven months ago, we enacted the biggest tax cuts and reforms in American history.

Our massive tax cuts provide tremendous relief for the middle class and small businesses.

To lower tax rates for hardworking Americans, we nearly doubled the standard deduction for everyone. Now, the first twenty-four thousand dollars earned by a married couple is completely tax-free. We also doubled the child tax credit.

A typical family of four making seventy-five thousand dollars will see their tax bill reduced by two thousand dollars—slashing their tax bill in half.

This April will be the last time you ever file under the old broken system—and millions of Americans will have more take-home pay starting next month.

We eliminated an especially cruel tax that fell mostly on Americans making less than fifty thousand dollars a year—forcing them to pay tremendous penalties simply because they could not afford government-ordered health plans. We repealed the core of disastrous Obamacare—the individual mandate is now gone.

We slashed the business tax rate from thirty-five percent all the way down to twenty-one percent, so American companies can compete and win against anyone in the world. These changes alone are estimated to increase average family income by more than four thousand dollars.

Small businesses have also received a massive tax cut, and can now deduct twenty percent of their business income.

Here tonight are Steve Staub and Sandy Keplinger of Staub Manufacturing—a small business in Ohio. They have just finished the best year in their twenty-year history. Because of tax reform, they are handing out raises, hiring an additional fourteen people, and expanding into the building next door.

One of Staub's employees, Corey Adams, is also with us tonight. Corey is an all-American worker. He supported himself through high school, lost his job during the 2008 recession, and was later hired by Staub, where he trained to become a welder. Like many hardworking Americans, Corey plans to invest his tax-cut raise into his new home and his two daughters' education. Please join me in congratulating Corey.

Since we passed tax cuts, roughly three million workers have already gotten tax-cut bonuses—many of them thousands of dollars per worker. Apple has just announced it plans to invest a total of $350 billion in America and hire another twenty-thousand workers. This is our new American moment. There has never been a better time to start living the American Dream. So to every citizen watching at home tonight—no matter where you have been, or where you come from, this is your time. If you work hard, if you believe in yourself, if you believe in America, then you can dream anything, you can be anything, and together, we can achieve anything.

Tonight, I want to talk about what kind of future we are going to have, and what kind of nation we are going to be. All of us, together, as one team, one people, and one American family.

We all share the same home, the same heart, the same destiny, and the same great American flag.

Together, we are rediscovering the American way.

In America, we know that faith and family, not government and bureaucracy, are the center of the American life. Our motto is "In God we trust."

And we celebrate our police, our military, and our amazing veterans as heroes who deserve our total and unwavering support.

Here tonight is Preston Sharp, a twelve-year-old boy from Redding, California, who noticed that veterans' graves were not marked with flags on Veterans' Day. He decided to change that, and started a movement that has now placed forty thousand flags at the graves of our great heroes. Preston: a job well done.

Young patriots like Preston teach all of us about our civic duty as Americans. Preston's reverence for those who have served our nation reminds us why we salute our flag, why we put our hands on our hearts for the Pledge of Allegiance, and why we proudly stand for the national anthem.

Americans love their country. And they deserve a government that shows them the same love and loyalty in return.

For the last year we have sought to restore the bonds of trust between our citizens and their government.

Working with the Senate, we are appointing judges who will interpret the Constitution as written, including a great new Supreme Court justice, and more circuit court judges than any new administration in the history of our country.

We are defending our Second Amendment, and have taken historic actions to protect religious liberty.

And we are serving our brave veterans, including giving our veterans choice in their healthcare decisions. Last year, the Congress passed, and I signed, the landmark VA Accountability

Act. Since its passage, my administration has already removed more than 1,500 VA employees who failed to give our veterans the care they deserve—and we are hiring talented people who love our vets as much as we do.

I will not stop until our veterans are properly taken care of, which has been my promise to them from the very beginning of this great journey.

All Americans deserve accountability and respect—and that is what we are giving them. So tonight, I call on the Congress to empower every Cabinet secretary with the authority to reward good workers—and to remove federal employees who undermine the public trust or fail the American people.

In our drive to make Washington accountable, we have eliminated more regulations in our first year than any administration in history.

We have ended the war on American energy—and we have ended the war on clean coal. We are now an exporter of energy to the world.

In Detroit, I halted government mandates that crippled America's autoworkers—so we can get the Motor City revving its engines once again.

Many car companies are now building and expanding plants in the United States—something we have not seen for decades. Chrysler is moving a major plant from Mexico to Michigan; Toyota and Mazda are opening up a plant in Alabama. Soon, plants will be opening up all over the country. This is all news Americans are unaccustomed to hearing—for many years, companies and jobs were only leaving us. But now they are coming back.

Exciting progress is happening every day.

To speed access to breakthrough cures and affordable generic drugs, last year the FDA approved more new and generic drugs and medical devices than ever before in our history.

We also believe that patients with terminal conditions should have access to experimental treatments that could potentially save their lives.

People who are terminally ill should not have to go from country to country to seek a cure—I want to give them a chance right here at home. It is time for the Congress to give these wonderful Americans the "right to try."

One of my greatest priorities is to reduce the price of prescription drugs. In many other countries, these drugs cost far less than what we pay in the United States. That is why I have directed my administration to make fixing the injustice of high drug prices one of our top priorities. Prices will come down.

America has also finally turned the page on decades of unfair trade deals that sacrificed our prosperity and shipped away our companies, our jobs, and our nation's wealth.

The era of economic surrender is over.

From now on, we expect trading relationships to be fair and to be reciprocal.

We will work to fix bad trade deals and negotiate new ones.

And we will protect American workers and American intellectual property, through strong enforcement of our trade rules.

As we rebuild our industries, it is also time to rebuild our crumbling infrastructure.

America is a nation of builders. We built the Empire State Building in just one year—is it not a disgrace that it can now take ten years just to get a permit approved for a simple road?

I am asking both parties to come together to give us the safe, fast, reliable, and modern infrastructure our economy needs and our people deserve.

Tonight, I am calling on the Congress to produce a bill that generates at least $1.5 trillion for the new infrastructure investment we need.

Every federal dollar should be leveraged by partnering with state and local governments and, where appropriate, tapping into private sector investment—to permanently fix the infrastructure deficit.

Any bill must also streamline the permitting and approval process—getting it down to no more than two years, and perhaps even one.

Together, we can reclaim our building heritage. We will build gleaming new roads, bridges, highways, railways, and waterways across our land. And we will do it with American heart, American hands, and American grit.

We want every American to know the dignity of a hard day's work. We want every child to be safe in their home at night. And we want every citizen to be proud of this land that we love.

We can lift our citizens from welfare to work, from dependence to independence, and from poverty to prosperity.

As tax cuts create new jobs, let us invest in workforce development and job training. Let us open great vocational schools so our future workers can learn a craft and realize their full potential. And let us support working families by supporting paid family leave.

As America regains its strength, this opportunity must be extended to all citizens. That is why this year we will embark on reforming our prisons to help former inmates who have served their time get a second chance.

Struggling communities, especially immigrant communities, will also be helped by immigration policies that focus on the best interests of American workers and American families.

For decades, open borders have allowed drugs and gangs to pour into our most vulnerable communities. They have allowed millions of low-wage workers to compete for jobs and wages against the poorest Americans. Most tragically, they have caused the loss of many innocent lives.

Here tonight are two fathers and two mothers: Evelyn Rodriguez, Freddy Cuevas, Elizabeth Alvarado, and Robert Mickens. Their two teenage daughters—Kayla Cuevas and Nisa Mickens—were close friends on Long Island. But in September 2016, on the eve of Nisa's sixteenth birthday, neither of them came home. These two precious girls were brutally murdered while walking together in their hometown. Six members of the savage gang MS-13 have been charged with Kayla and Nisa's murders. Many of these gang members took advantage of glaring loopholes in our laws to enter the country as unaccompanied alien minors—and wound up in Kayla and Nisa's high school.

Evelyn, Elizabeth, Freddy, and Robert: tonight, everyone in this chamber is praying for you. Everyone in America is grieving for you. And 320 million hearts are breaking for you. We cannot imagine the depth of your sorrow, but we can make sure that other families never have to endure this pain.

Tonight, I am calling on the Congress to finally close the deadly loopholes that have allowed MS-13 and other criminals to break into our country. We have proposed new legislation that will fix our immigration laws, and support our ICE and border patrol agents, so that this cannot ever happen again.

The United States is a compassionate nation. We are proud that we do more than any other country to help the needy, the struggling, and the underprivileged all over the world. But as president of the United States, my highest loyalty, my greatest compassion, and my constant concern is for America's children, America's struggling workers, and America's forgotten communities. I want our youth to grow up to achieve great things. I want our poor to have their chance to rise.

So tonight, I am extending an open hand to work with members of both parties—Democrats and Republicans—to protect our citizens of every background, color, religion, and creed. My duty, and the sacred duty of every elected official in this chamber, is to defend Americans—to protect their safety, their families, their communities, and their right to the American Dream. Because Americans are dreamers too.

Here tonight is one leader in the effort to defend our country: Homeland Security Investigations special agent Celestino Martinez—he goes by CJ. CJ served fifteen years in the Air Force before becoming an ICE agent and spending the last fifteen years fighting gang violence and getting dangerous criminals off our streets. At one point, MS-13 leaders ordered CJ's murder. But he did not cave to threats or fear. Last May, he commanded an operation to track down gang members on Long Island. His team has arrested nearly 400, including more than 220 from MS-13.

CJ: Great work. Now let us get the Congress to send you some reinforcements.

Over the next few weeks, the House and Senate will be voting on an immigration reform package.

In recent months, my administration has met extensively with both Democrats and Republicans to craft a bipartisan approach to immigration reform. Based on these discussions, we presented the Congress with a detailed proposal that should be supported by both parties as a fair compromise—one where nobody gets everything they want, but where our country gets the critical reforms it needs.

Here are the four pillars of our plan:

The first pillar of our framework generously offers a path to citizenship for 1.8 million illegal immigrants who were brought here by their parents at a young age—that covers almost three times more people than the previous administration. Under our plan, those who meet education and work requirements and show good moral character will be able to become full citizens of the United States.

The second pillar fully secures the border. That means building a wall on the southern border, and it means hiring more heroes like CJ to keep our communities safe. Crucially, our plan closes the terrible loopholes exploited by criminals and terrorists to enter our country—and it finally ends the dangerous practice of "catch and release."

The third pillar ends the visa lottery—a program that randomly hands out green cards without any regard for skill, merit, or the safety of our people. It is time to begin moving towards a merit-based immigration system—one that admits people who are skilled, who want to work, who will contribute to our society, and who will love and respect our country.

The fourth and final pillar protects the nuclear family by ending chain migration. Under the current broken system, a single immigrant can bring in virtually unlimited numbers of distant relatives. Under our plan, we focus on the immediate family by limiting sponsorships to spouses and minor children. This vital reform is necessary, not just for our economy, but for our security and our future.

In recent weeks, two terrorist attacks in New York were made possible by the visa lottery and chain migration. In the age of terrorism, these programs present risks we can no longer afford.

It is time to reform these outdated immigration rules, and finally bring our immigration system into the twenty-first century.

These four pillars represent a down-the-middle compromise, and one that will create a safe, modern, and lawful immigration system.

For over thirty years, Washington has tried and failed to solve this problem. This Congress can be the one that finally makes it happen.

Most importantly, these four pillars will produce legislation that fulfills my ironclad pledge to only sign a bill that puts America first. So let us come together, set politics aside, and finally get the job done.

These reforms will also support our response to the terrible crisis of opioid and drug addiction.

In 2016, we lost sixty-four thousand Americans to drug overdoses: 174 deaths per day. Seven per hour. We must get much tougher on drug dealers and pushers if we are going to succeed in stopping this scourge.

My administration is committed to fighting the drug epidemic and helping get treatment for those in need. The struggle will be long and difficult—but, as Americans always do, we will prevail.

As we have seen tonight, the most difficult challenges bring out the best in America.

We see a vivid expression of this truth in the story of the Holets family of New Mexico. Ryan Holets is twenty-seven years old and an officer with the Albuquerque Police Department. He is here tonight with his wife, Rebecca. Last year, Ryan was on duty when he saw a pregnant, homeless woman preparing to inject heroin. When Ryan told her she was going to harm her unborn child, she began to weep. She told him she did not know where to turn but badly wanted a safe home for her baby.

In that moment, Ryan said he felt God speak to him: "You will do it—because you can." He took out a picture of his wife and their four kids. Then, he went home to tell his wife, Rebecca. In an instant, she agreed to adopt. The Holets named their new daughter Hope.

Ryan and Rebecca: you embody the goodness of our nation. Thank you, and congratulations.

As we rebuild America's strength and confidence at home, we are also restoring our strength and standing abroad.

Around the world, we face rogue regimes, terrorist groups, and rivals like China and Russia that challenge our interests, our economy, and our values. In confronting these dangers, we know that weakness is the surest path to conflict, and unmatched power is the surest means of our defense.

For this reason, I am asking the Congress to end the dangerous defense sequester and fully fund our great military.

As part of our defense, we must modernize and rebuild our nuclear arsenal, hopefully never having to use it, but making it so strong and powerful that it will deter any acts of aggression. Perhaps someday in the future there will be a magical moment when the countries of the world will get together to eliminate their nuclear weapons. Unfortunately, we are not there yet.

Last year, I also pledged that we would work with our allies to extinguish ISIS from the face of the earth. One year later, I am proud to report that the coalition to defeat ISIS has liberated almost 100 percent of the territory once held by these killers in Iraq and Syria. But there is much more work to be done. We will continue our fight until ISIS is defeated.

Army staff sergeant Justin Peck is here tonight. Near Raqqa last November, Justin and his comrade, Chief Petty Officer Kenton Stacy, were on a mission to clear buildings that ISIS had rigged with explosives so that civilians could return to the city.

Clearing the second floor of a vital hospital, Kenton Stacy was severely wounded by an explosion. Immediately, Justin bounded into the booby-trapped building and found Kenton in bad shape. He applied pressure to the wound and inserted a tube to reopen an airway. He then performed CPR for twenty straight minutes during the ground transport and maintained artificial respiration through two hours of emergency surgery.

Kenton Stacy would have died if not for Justin's selfless love for a fellow warrior. Tonight, Kenton is recovering in Texas. Raqqa is liberated. And Justin is wearing his new Bronze Star, with a "V" for "valor." Staff Sergeant Peck: all of America salutes you.

Terrorists who do things like place bombs in civilian hospitals are evil. When possible, we annihilate them. When necessary, we must be able to detain and question them. But we must be clear: terrorists are not merely criminals. They are unlawful enemy combatants. And when captured overseas, they should be treated like the terrorists they are.

In the past, we have foolishly released hundreds of dangerous terrorists, only to meet them again on the battle-field—including the ISIS leader al-Baghdadi.

So today, I am keeping another promise. I just signed an order directing Secretary Mattis to reexamine our military detention policy and to keep open the detention facilities at Guantánamo Bay.

I am also asking the Congress to ensure that, in the fight against ISIS and al-Qa'ida, we continue to have all necessary power to detain terrorists—wherever we chase them down.

Our warriors in Afghanistan also have new rules of engage-ment. Along with their heroic Afghan partners, our military is no longer undermined by artificial timelines, and we no longer tell our enemies our plans.

Last month, I also took an action endorsed unanimously by the Senate just months before: I recognized Jerusalem as the capital of Israel.

Shortly afterwards, dozens of countries voted in the United Nations General Assembly against America's sovereign right to make this recognition. American taxpayers generously send those same countries billions of dollars in aid every year.

That is why, tonight, I am asking the Congress to pass legislation to help ensure American foreign-assistance dol-lars always serve American interests, and only go to America's friends.

As we strengthen friendships around the world, we are also restoring clarity about our adversaries.

When the people of Iran rose up against the crimes of their corrupt dictatorship, I did not stay silent. America stands with the people of Iran in their courageous struggle for freedom.

I am asking the Congress to address the fundamental flaws in the terrible Iran nuclear deal.

My administration has also imposed tough sanctions on the communist and socialist dictatorships in Cuba and Venezuela.

But no regime has oppressed its own citizens more totally or brutally than the cruel dictatorship in North Korea.

North Korea's reckless pursuit of nuclear missiles could very soon threaten our homeland.

We are waging a campaign of maximum pressure to prevent that from happening.

Past experience has taught us that complacency and concessions only invite aggression and provocation. I will not repeat the mistakes of past administrations that got us into this dangerous position.

We need only look at the depraved character of the North Korean regime to understand the nature of the nuclear threat it could pose to America and our allies.

Otto Warmbier was a hardworking student at the University of Virginia. On his way to study abroad in Asia, Otto joined a tour to North Korea. At its conclusion, this wonderful young man was arrested and charged with crimes against the state. After a shameful trial, the dictatorship sentenced Otto to fifteen years of hard labor, before returning him to America last June— horribly injured and on the verge of death. He passed away just days after his return.

Otto's parents, Fred and Cindy Warmbier, are with us tonight—along with Otto's brother and sister, Austin and Greta. You are powerful witnesses to a menace that threatens our world, and your strength inspires us all. Tonight, we pledge to honor Otto's memory with American resolve.

Finally, we are joined by one more witness to the ominous nature of this regime. His name is Mr. Ji Seong-ho.

In 1996, Seong-ho was a starving boy in North Korea. One day, he tried to steal coal from a railroad car to barter for a few scraps of food. In the process, he passed out on the train tracks, exhausted from hunger. He woke up as a train ran over his limbs. He then endured multiple amputations without anything to dull the pain. His brother and sister gave what little food they had to help him recover and ate dirt themselves—permanently stunting their own growth. Later, he was tortured by North Korean authorities after returning from a brief visit to China. His tormentors wanted to know if he had met any Christians. He had—and he resolved to be free.

Seong-ho traveled thousands of miles on crutches across China and Southeast Asia to freedom. Most of his family followed. His father was caught trying to escape, and was tortured to death.

Today he lives in Seoul, where he rescues other defectors and broadcasts into North Korea what the regime fears the most—the truth.

Today he has a new leg, but Seong-ho, I understand you still keep those crutches as a reminder of how far you have come. Your great sacrifice is an inspiration to us all.

Seong-ho's story is a testament to the yearning of every human soul to live in freedom.

It was that same yearning for freedom that nearly 250 years ago gave birth to a special place called America. It was a small cluster of colonies caught between a great ocean and a vast wilderness. But it was home to an incredible people with a revolutionary idea: that they could rule themselves. That they could chart their own destiny. And that, together, they could light up the world.

That is what our country has always been about. That is what Americans have always stood for, always strived for, and always done.

Atop the dome of this Capitol stands the Statue of Freedom. She stands tall and dignified among the monuments to our ancestors who fought and lived and died to protect her.

Monuments to Washington and Jefferson—to Lincoln and King.

Memorials to the heroes of Yorktown and Saratoga—to young Americans who shed their blood on the shores of Normandy and the fields beyond. And others, who went down in the waters of the Pacific and the skies over Asia.

And freedom stands tall over one more monument: this one. This Capitol. This living monument to the American people.

A people whose heroes live not only in the past but all around us—defending hope, pride, and the American way.

They work in every trade. They sacrifice to raise a family. They care for our children at home. They defend our flag abroad. They are strong moms and brave kids. They are firefighters, police officers, border agents, medics, and Marines.

But above all else, they are Americans. And this Capitol, this city, and this nation, belong to them.

Our task is to respect them, to listen to them, to serve them, to protect them, and to always be worthy of them.

Americans fill the world with art and music. They push the bounds of science and discovery. And they forever remind us of what we should never forget: the people dreamed this country. The people built this country. And it is the people who are making America great again.

As long as we are proud of who we are, and what we are fighting for, there is nothing we cannot achieve.

As long as we have confidence in our values, faith in our citizens, and trust in our God, we will not fail.

Our families will thrive.

Our people will prosper.

And our nation will forever be safe and strong and proud and mighty and free.

Thank you, and God bless America.[171]

President Donald Trump's Inaugural Address

January 20, 2017
Remarks as prepared for delivery.

Chief Justice Roberts, President Carter, President Clinton, President Bush, President Obama, fellow Americans, and people of the world: thank you.

We, the citizens of America, are now joined in a great national effort to rebuild our country and to restore its promise for all of our people.

---

[171]   https://www.whitehouse.gov/briefings-statements/president-donald-j-trumps-state-union-address/

Together, we will determine the course of America and the world for years to come.

We will face challenges. We will confront hardships. But we will get the job done.

Every four years, we gather on these steps to carry out the orderly and peaceful transfer of power, and we are grateful to President Obama and First Lady Michelle Obama for their gracious aid throughout this transition. They have been magnificent.

Today's ceremony, however, has very special meaning. Because today we are not merely transferring power from one administration to another, or from one party to another—but we are transferring power from Washington, D.C., and giving it back to you, the American people.

For too long, a small group in our nation's capital has reaped the rewards of government while the people have borne the cost.

Washington flourished—but the people did not share in its wealth.

Politicians prospered—but the jobs left, and the factories closed.

The establishment protected itself but not the citizens of our country.

Their victories have not been your victories; their triumphs have not been your triumphs; and while they celebrated in our nation's capital, there was little to celebrate for struggling families all across our land.

That all changes—starting right here, and right now, because this moment is your moment: it belongs to you.

It belongs to everyone gathered here today and everyone watching all across America.

This is your day. This is your celebration.

And this, the United States of America, is your country.

What truly matters is not which party controls our government, but whether our government is controlled by the people.

January 20, 2017, will be remembered as the day the people became the rulers of this nation again.

The forgotten men and women of our country will be forgotten no longer.

Everyone is listening to you now.

You came by the tens of millions to become part of a historic movement the likes of which the world has never seen before.

At the center of this movement is a crucial conviction: that a nation exists to serve its citizens.

Americans want great schools for their children, safe neighborhoods for their families, and good jobs for themselves.

These are the just and reasonable demands of a righteous public.

But for too many of our citizens, a different reality exists: mothers and children trapped in poverty in our inner cities; rusted-out factories scattered like tombstones across the landscape of our nation; an education system flush with cash but which leaves our young and beautiful students deprived of knowledge; and the crime and gangs and drugs that have stolen too many lives and robbed our country of so much unrealized potential.

This American carnage stops right here and stops right now.

We are one nation—and their pain is our pain. Their dreams are our dreams; and their success will be our success. We share one heart, one home, and one glorious destiny.

The oath of office I take today is an oath of allegiance to all Americans.

For many decades, we've enriched foreign industry at the expense of American industry; subsidized the armies of other countries while allowing for the very sad depletion of our military.

We've defended other nation's borders while refusing to defend our own, and spent trillions of dollars overseas while America's infrastructure has fallen into disrepair and decay.

We've made other countries rich while the wealth, strength, and confidence of our country has disappeared over the horizon.

One by one, the factories shuttered and left our shores, with not even a thought about the millions upon millions of American workers left behind.

The wealth of our middle class has been ripped from their homes and then redistributed across the entire world.

But that is the past. And now we are looking only to the future.

We assembled here today are issuing a new decree to be heard in every city, in every foreign capital, and in every hall of power.

From this day forward, a new vision will govern our land.

From this moment on, it's going to be America first.

Every decision on trade, on taxes, on immigration, on foreign affairs will be made to benefit American workers and American families.

We must protect our borders from the ravages of other countries making our products, stealing our companies, and destroying our jobs. Protection will lead to great prosperity and strength.

I will fight for you with every breath in my body—and I will never, ever let you down.

America will start winning again, winning like never before.

We will bring back our jobs. We will bring back our borders. We will bring back our wealth. And we will bring back our dreams.

We will build new roads, and highways, and bridges, and airports, and tunnels, and railways all across our wonderful nation.

We will get our people off of welfare and back to work—rebuilding our country with American hands and American labor.

We will follow two simple rules: buy American and hire American.

We will seek friendship and goodwill with the nations of the world—but we do so with the understanding that it is the right of all nations to put their own interests first.

We do not seek to impose our way of life on anyone, but rather to let it shine as an example for everyone to follow.

We will reinforce old alliances and form new ones—and unite the civilized world against radical Islamic terrorism, which we will eradicate completely from the face of the earth.

At the bedrock of our politics will be a total allegiance to the United States of America, and through our loyalty to our country, we will rediscover our loyalty to each other.

When you open your heart to patriotism, there is no room for prejudice.

The Bible tells us, "How good and pleasant it is when God's people live together in unity."

We must speak our minds openly, debate our disagreements honestly, but always pursue solidarity.

When America is united, America is totally unstoppable.

There should be no fear—we are protected, and we will always be protected.

We will be protected by the great men and women of our military and law enforcement and, most importantly, we are protected by God.

Finally, we must think big and dream even bigger.

In America, we understand that a nation is only living as long as it is striving.

We will no longer accept politicians who are all talk and no action—constantly complaining but never doing anything about it.

The time for empty talk is over.

Now arrives the hour of action.

Do not let anyone tell you it cannot be done. No challenge can match the heart and fight and spirit of America.

We will not fail. Our country will thrive and prosper again.

We stand at the birth of a new millennium, ready to unlock the mysteries of space, to free the earth from the miseries of disease, and to harness the energies, industries, and technologies of tomorrow.

A new national pride will stir our souls, lift our sights, and heal our divisions.

It is time to remember that old wisdom our soldiers will never forget: that whether we are black or brown or white, we all bleed the same red blood of patriots, we all enjoy the same glorious freedoms, and we all salute the same great American flag.

And whether a child is born in the urban sprawl of Detroit or the windswept plains of Nebraska, they look up at the same night sky, they fill their heart with the same dreams, and they are infused with the breath of life by the same almighty Creator.

So to all Americans, in every city near and far, small and large, from mountain to mountain, and from ocean to ocean, hear these words:

You will never be ignored again.

Your voice, your hopes, and your dreams will define our American destiny. And your courage and goodness and love will forever guide us along the way.

Together, we will make America strong again.

We will make America wealthy again.

We will make America proud again.

We will make America safe again.

And, yes, together we will make America great again. Thank you, God bless you, and God bless America.[172]

President Ronald Reagan's Inaugural Address

January 20, 1981

Remarks as prepared for delivery.

Senator Hatfield, Mr. Chief Justice, Mr. President, Vice President Bush, Vice President Mondale, Senator Baker, Speaker O'Neill, Reverend Moomaw, and my fellow citizens:

---

[172] https://www.whitehouse.gov/briefings-statements/the-inaugural-address/

To a few of us here today this is a solemn and most momentous occasion, and yet in the history of our nation it is a commonplace occurrence. The orderly transfer of authority as called for in the Constitution routinely takes place, as it has for almost two centuries, and few of us stop to think how unique we really are. In the eyes of many in the world, this every-four-year ceremony we accept as normal is nothing less than a miracle.

Mr. President, I want our fellow citizens to know how much you did to carry on this tradition. By your gracious cooperation in the transition process, you have shown a watching world that we are a united people pledged to maintaining a political system which guarantees individual liberty to a greater degree than any other, and I thank you and your people for all your help in maintaining the continuity which is the bulwark of our republic.

The business of our nation goes forward. These United States are confronted with an economic affliction of great proportions. We suffer from the longest and one of the worst sustained inflations in our national history. It distorts our economic decisions, penalizes thrift, and crushes the struggling young and the fixed-income elderly alike. It threatens to shatter the lives of millions of our people.

Idle industries have cast workers into unemployment, human misery, and personal indignity. Those who do work are denied a fair return for their labor by a tax system which penalizes successful achievement and keeps us from maintaining full productivity.

But great as our tax burden is, it has not kept pace with public spending. For decades we have piled deficit upon deficit, mortgaging our future and our children's future for the temporary convenience of the present. To continue this long trend is to guarantee tremendous social, cultural, political, and economic upheavals.

You and I, as individuals, can, by borrowing, live beyond our means, but for only a limited period of time. Why, then, should we think that collectively, as a nation, we're not bound by that same limitation? We must act today in order to preserve tomorrow. And let there be no misunderstanding: we are going to begin to act, beginning today.

The economic ills we suffer have come upon us over several decades. They will not go away in days, weeks, or months, but they will go away. They will go away because we as Americans have the capacity now, as we've had in the past, to do whatever needs to be done to preserve this last and greatest bastion of freedom.

In this present crisis, government is not the solution to our problem; government is the problem. From time to time we've been tempted to believe that society has become too complex to be managed by self-rule, that government by an elite group is superior to government for, by, and of the people. Well, if no one among us is capable of governing himself, then who among us has the capacity to govern someone else? All of us together, in and out of government, must bear the burden. The solutions we seek must be equitable, with no one group singled out to pay a higher price.

We hear much of special interest groups. Well, our concern must be for a special interest group that has been too long neglected. It knows no sectional boundaries or ethnic and racial divisions, and it crosses political party lines. It is made up of men and women who raise our food, patrol our streets, man our mines and factories, teach our children, keep our homes, and heal us when we're sick—professionals, industrialists, shopkeepers, clerks, cabbies, and truckdrivers. They are, in short, "We the people," this breed called Americans.

Well, this administration's objective will be a healthy, vigorous, growing economy that provides equal opportunities for all Americans with no barriers born of bigotry or discrimination. Putting America back to work means putting all Americans back to work. Ending inflation means freeing all Americans from the terror of runaway living costs. All must share in the productive work of this "new beginning," and all must share in the bounty of a revived economy. With the idealism and fair play which are the core of our system and our strength, we can have a strong and prosperous America, at peace with itself and the world.

So, as we begin, let us take inventory. We are a nation that has a government—not the other way around. And this makes us special among the nations of the earth. Our government has no power except that granted it by the people. It is time to check and reverse the growth of government, which shows signs of having grown beyond the consent of the governed.

It is my intention to curb the size and influence of the federal establishment and to demand recognition of the distinction between the powers granted to the federal government and those reserved to the states or to the people. All of us need to be reminded that the federal government did not create the states; the states created the federal government.

Now, so there will be no misunderstanding, it's not my intention to do away with government. It is rather to make it work—work with us, not over us; to stand by our side, not ride on our back. Government can and must provide opportunity, not smother it; foster productivity, not stifle it.

If we look to the answer as to why for so many years we achieved so much, prospered as no other people on Earth, it was because here in this land we unleashed the energy and individual genius of man to a greater extent than has ever been done before. Freedom and the dignity of the individual have been more available and assured here than in any other place on Earth. The price for this freedom at times has been high, but we have never been unwilling to pay that price.

It is no coincidence that our present troubles parallel and are proportionate to the intervention and intrusion in our lives that result from unnecessary and excessive growth of government. It is time for us to realize that we're too great a nation to limit ourselves to small dreams. We're not, as some would have us believe, doomed to an inevitable decline. I do not believe in a fate that will fall on us no matter what we do. I do believe in a fate that will fall on us if we do nothing. So, with all the creative energy at our command, let us begin an era of national renewal. Let us renew our determination, our courage, and our strength. And let us renew our faith and our hope.

We have every right to dream heroic dreams. Those who say that we're in a time when there are not heroes, they just don't know where to look. You can see heroes every day going in and out of factory gates. Others, a handful in number, produce enough food to feed all of us and then the world beyond. You meet heroes across a counter, and they're on both sides of that counter. There are entrepreneurs with faith in themselves and faith in an idea who create new jobs, new wealth, and opportunity. They're individuals and families whose taxes support the government and whose voluntary gifts support church, charity, culture, art, and education. Their patriotism is quiet but deep. Their values sustain our national life.

Now, I have used the words "they" and "their" in speaking of these heroes. I could say "you" and "your," because I'm addressing the heroes of whom I speak—you, the citizens of this blessed land. Your dreams, your hopes, your goals are going to be the dreams, the hopes, and the goals of this administration, so help me God.

We shall reflect the compassion that is so much a part of your makeup. How can we love our country and not love our countrymen; and loving them, reach out a hand when they fall, heal them when they're sick, and provide opportunity to make them self-sufficient so they will be equal in fact and not just in theory?

Can we solve the problems confronting us? Well, the answer is an unequivocal and emphatic "yes." To paraphrase Winston Churchill, I did not take the oath I've just taken with the intention of presiding over the dissolution of the world's strongest economy.

In the days ahead I will propose removing the roadblocks that have slowed our economy and reduced productivity. Steps will be taken aimed at restoring the balance between the various levels of government. Progress may be slow, measured in inches and feet, not miles, but we will progress. It is time to reawaken this industrial giant, to get government back within its means, and to lighten our punitive tax burden. And these will be our first priorities, and on these principles there will be no compromise.

On the eve of our struggle for independence a man who might have been one of the greatest among the Founding Fathers, Dr. Joseph Warren, president of the Massachusetts Congress, said to his fellow Americans, "Our country is in danger, but not to be despaired of.... On you depend the fortunes of America. You are to decide the important questions upon which rests the happiness and the liberty of millions yet unborn. Act worthy of yourselves."

Well, I believe we, the Americans of today, are ready to act worthy of ourselves, ready to do what must be done to ensure happiness and liberty for ourselves, our children, and our children's children. And as we renew ourselves here in our own land, we will be seen as having greater strength throughout the world. We will again be the exemplar of freedom and a beacon of hope for those who do not now have freedom.

To those neighbors and allies who share our freedom, we will strengthen our historic ties and assure them of our support and firm commitment. We will match loyalty with loyalty. We will strive for mutually beneficial relations. We will not use our friendship to impose on their sovereignty, for our own sovereignty is not for sale.

As for the enemies of freedom, those who are potential adversaries, they will be reminded that peace is the highest aspiration of the American people. We will negotiate for it, sacrifice for it; we will not surrender for it, now or ever.

Our forbearance should never be misunderstood. Our reluctance for conflict should not be misjudged as a failure of will. When action is required to preserve our national security, we will act. We will maintain sufficient strength to prevail if need be, knowing that if we do so we have the best chance of never having to use that strength.

Above all, we must realize that no arsenal or no weapon in the arsenals of the world is so formidable as the will and moral courage of free men and women. It is a weapon our adversaries in today's world do not have. It is a weapon that we as Americans do have. Let that be understood by those who practice terrorism and prey upon their neighbors.

I'm told that tens of thousands of prayer meetings are being held on this day, and for that I'm deeply grateful. We are a nation under God, and I believe God intended for us to be free. It would be fitting and good, I think, if on each Inaugural Day in future years it should be declared a day of prayer.

This is the first time in our history that this ceremony has been held, as you've been told, on this West Front of the Capitol. Standing here, one faces a magnificent vista, opening up on this city's special beauty and history. At the end of this open mall are those shrines to the giants on whose shoulders we stand.

Directly in front of me, the monument to a monumental man, George Washington, father of our country. A man of humility who came to greatness reluctantly. He led America out of revolutionary victory into infant nationhood. Off to one side, the stately memorial to Thomas Jefferson. The Declaration of Independence flames with his eloquence. And then, beyond the Reflecting Pool, the dignified columns of the Lincoln Memorial. Whoever would understand in his heart the meaning of America will find it in the life of Abraham Lincoln.

Beyond those monuments to heroism is the Potomac River, and on the far shore the sloping hills of Arlington National Cemetery, with its row upon row of simple white markers bearing crosses or Stars of David. They add up to only a tiny fraction of the price that has been paid for our freedom.

Each one of those markers is a monument to the kind of hero I spoke of earlier. Their lives ended in places called Belleau Wood, The Argonne, Omaha Beach, Salerno, and halfway around the world on Guadalcanal, Tarawa, Pork Chop Hill, the Chosin Reservoir, and in a hundred rice paddies and jungles of a place called Vietnam.

Under one such marker lies a young man, Martin Treptow, who left his job in a small town barbershop in 1917 to go to France with the famed Rainbow Division. There, on the western front, he was killed trying to carry a message between battalions under heavy artillery fire.

We're told that on his body was found a diary. On the flyleaf under the heading "My Pledge," he had written these words: "America must win this war. Therefore I will work, I will save, I will sacrifice, I will endure, I will fight cheerfully and do my utmost, as if the issue of the whole struggle depended on me alone."

The crisis we are facing today does not require of us the kind of sacrifice that Martin Treptow and so many thousands of others were called upon to make. It does require, however, our best effort and our willingness to believe in ourselves and to believe in our capacity to perform great deeds, to believe that together with God's help we can and will resolve the problems which now confront us.

And after all, why shouldn't we believe that? We are Americans.

God bless you, and thank you.[173]

President Ronald Reagan's Remarks on East-West Relations

Brandenburg Gate, West Berlin
June 12, 1987
Remarks as prepared for delivery.

Thank you very much. Chancellor Kohl, Governing Mayor Diepgen, ladies and gentlemen:

Twenty four years ago, President John F. Kennedy visited Berlin, speaking to the people of this city and the world at the city hall. Well, since then two other presidents have come, each in his turn, to Berlin. And today I, myself, make my second visit to your city. We come to Berlin, we American presidents, because it's our duty to speak, in this place, of freedom. But I must confess, we're drawn here by other things as well: by the feeling of history in this city, more than five hundred years older than our own nation; by the beauty of the Grunewald and the Tiergarten; most of all, by your courage and determination. Perhaps the composer Paul Lincke understood something about American presidents.

You see, like so many presidents before me, I come here today because wherever I go, whatever I do: "*Ich hab noch einen Koffer in Berlin.*" (I still have a suitcase in Berlin.) Our gathering today is being broadcast throughout Western Europe and North America. I understand that it is being seen and heard as well in the East. To those listening throughout Eastern Europe,

---

[173] https://www.reaganlibrary.gov/research/speeches/inaugural-address-january-20-1981

I extend my warmest greetings and the goodwill of the American people. To those listening in East Berlin, a special word: although I cannot be with you, I address my remarks to you just as surely as to those standing here before me. For I join you, as I join your fellow countrymen in the West, in this firm, this unalterable belief: *es gibt nur ein Berlin*. (There is only one Berlin.)

Behind me stands a wall that encircles the free sectors of this city, part of a vast system of barriers that divides the entire continent of Europe. From the Baltic south, those barriers cut across Germany in a gash of barbed wire, concrete, dog runs, and guard towers. Farther south, there may be no visible, no obvious wall. But there remain armed guards and checkpoints all the same—still a restriction on the right to travel, still an instrument to impose upon ordinary men and women the will of a totalitarian state.

Yet it is here in Berlin where the wall emerges most clearly; here, cutting across your city, where the news photo and the television screen have imprinted this brutal division of a continent upon the mind of the world. Standing before the Brandenburg Gate, every man is a German, separated from his fellow men. Every man is a Berliner, forced to look upon a scar. President von Weizsacker has said: "The German question is open as long as the Brandenburg Gate is closed." Today I say: as long as this gate is closed, as long as this scar of a wall is permitted to stand, it is not the German question alone that remains open, but the question of freedom for all mankind.

Yet I do not come here to lament. For I find in Berlin a message of hope, even in the shadow of this wall, a message of triumph. In this season of spring in 1945, the people of Berlin emerged from their air raid shelters to find devastation.

Thousands of miles away, the people of the United States reached out to help. And in 1947 Secretary of State—as you've been told—George Marshall announced the creation of what would become known as the Marshall Plan. Speaking precisely forty years ago this month, he said: "Our policy is directed not against any country or doctrine, but against hunger, poverty, desperation, and chaos."

In the Reichstag a few moments ago, I saw a display commemorating this fortieth anniversary of the Marshall Plan. I was struck by the sign on a burnt-out, gutted structure that was being rebuilt. I understand that Berliners of my own generation can remember seeing signs like it dotted throughout the Western sectors of the city. The sign read simply: "The Marshall Plan is helping here to strengthen the free world." A strong, free world in the West, that dream became real. Japan rose from ruin to become an economic giant. Italy, France, Belgium—virtually every nation in Western Europe saw political and economic rebirth; the European Community was founded.

In West Germany and here in Berlin, there took place an economic miracle, the Wirtschaftswunder. Adenauer, Erhard, Reuter, and other leaders understood the practical importance of liberty—that just as truth can flourish only when the journalist is given freedom of speech, so prosperity can come about only when the farmer and businessman enjoy economic freedom. The German leaders reduced tariffs, expanded free trade, lowered taxes.

From 1950 to 1960 alone, the standard of living in West Germany and Berlin doubled. Where four decades ago there was rubble, today in West Berlin there is the greatest industrial output of any city in Germany—busy office blocks, fine homes and apartments, proud avenues, and the spreading lawns of parkland. Where a city's culture seemed to have been destroyed, today there are two great universities, orchestras and an opera, countless theaters, and museums. Where there was want, today there's abundance—food, clothing, automobiles—the wonderful goods of the Ku'damm. From devastation, from utter ruin, you Berliners have, in freedom, rebuilt a city that once again ranks as one of the greatest on Earth. The Soviets may have had other plans. But, my friends, there were a few things the Soviets didn't count on: Berliner *Herz*, Berliner humor, *ja*, und Berliner *Schnauze*. (Berliner heart, Berliner humor, yes, and a Berliner *Schnauze*.) In the 1950s, Khrushchev predicted: "We will bury you." But in the West today, we see a free world that has achieved a level of prosperity and well-being unprecedented in all human history. In the Communist world, we see failure, technological backwardness, declining standards of health, even want of the most basic kind—too little food. Even today, the Soviet Union still cannot feed itself.

After these four decades, then, there stands before the entire world one great and inescapable conclusion: freedom leads to prosperity. Freedom replaces the ancient hatreds among the nations with comity and peace. Freedom is the victor. And now the Soviets themselves may, in a limited way, be coming to understand the importance of freedom. We hear much from Moscow about a new policy of reform and openness. Some political prisoners have been released. Certain foreign news broadcasts are no longer being jammed. Some economic enterprises have been permitted to operate with greater freedom from state control. Are these the beginnings of profound changes in the Soviet state? Or are they token gestures, intended to raise false hopes in the West, or to strengthen the Soviet system without changing it? We welcome change and openness; for we believe that freedom and security go together, that the advance of human liberty can only strengthen the cause of world peace. There is one sign the Soviets can make that would be unmistakable, that would advance dramatically the cause of freedom and peace. General Secretary Gorbachev, if you seek peace, if you seek prosperity for the Soviet Union and Eastern Europe, if you seek liberalization: come here to this gate! Mr. Gorbachev, open this gate! Mr. Gorbachev, tear down this wall! I understand the fear of war and the pain of division that afflict this continent—and I pledge to you my country's efforts to help overcome these burdens.

To be sure, we in the West must resist Soviet expansion. So we must maintain defenses of unassailable strength. Yet we seek peace; so we must strive to reduce arms on both sides. Beginning ten years ago, the Soviets challenged the Western alliance with a grave new threat, hundreds of new and more deadly SS20 nuclear missiles, capable of striking every capital in Europe. The Western alliance responded by committing itself to a counterdeployment unless the Soviets agreed to negotiate a better solution; namely, the elimination of such weapons on both sides. For many months, the Soviets refused to bargain in earnestness. As the alliance, in turn, prepared to go forward with its counterdeployment, there were difficult days—days of protests, like those during my 1982 visit to this city—and the Soviets later walked away from the table. But through it all, the alliance held firm. And I invite those who protested then—I invite those who protest today—to mark this fact: because we remained strong, the Soviets came back to the table. And because we remained strong, today we have within reach the possibility, not merely of limiting the growth of arms, but of eliminating, for the first time, an entire class of nuclear weapons from the face of the earth.

As I speak, NATO ministers are meeting in Iceland to review the progress of our proposals for eliminating these weapons. At the talks in Geneva, we have also proposed deep cuts in strategic offensive weapons. And the Western allies have likewise made far-reaching proposals to reduce the danger of conventional war and to place a total ban on chemical weapons. While we pursue these arms reductions, I pledge to you that we will maintain the capacity to deter Soviet aggression at any level at which it might occur. And in cooperation with many of our allies, the United States is pursuing the Strategic Defense Initiative research to base deterrence not on the threat of offensive retaliation, but on defenses that truly defend; on systems, in short, that will not target populations but shield them. By these means we seek to increase the safety of Europe and all the world. But we must remember a crucial fact: East and West do not mistrust each other because we are armed; we are armed because we mistrust each other. And our differences are not about weapons but about liberty.

When President Kennedy spoke at the City Hall those twenty-four years ago, freedom was encircled; Berlin was under siege. And today, despite all the pressures upon this city, Berlin stands secure in its liberty. And freedom itself is transforming the globe. In the Philippines, in South and Central America, democracy has been given a rebirth. Throughout the Pacific, free markets are working miracle after miracle of economic growth. In the industrialized nations, a technological revolution is taking place—a revolution marked by rapid, dramatic advances in computers and telecommunications. In Europe, only one nation and those it controls refuse to join the community of freedom.

Yet in this age of redoubled economic growth, of information and innovation, the Soviet Union faces a choice: it must make fundamental changes, or it will become obsolete. Today thus represents a moment of hope. We in the West stand ready to cooperate with the East to promote true openness, to break down barriers that separate people, to create a safer, freer world. And surely there is no better place than Berlin, the meeting place of East and West, to make a start. Free people of Berlin: today, as in the past, the United States stands for the strict observance and full implementation of all parts of the Four Power Agreement of 1971.

Let us use this occasion, the 750th anniversary of this city, to usher in a new era, to seek a still fuller, richer life for the Berlin of the future. Together, let us maintain and develop the ties between the Federal Republic and the western sectors of Berlin, which is permitted by the 1971 agreement. And I invite Mr. Gorbachev: let us work to bring the eastern and western parts of the city closer together, so that all the inhabitants of all Berlin can enjoy the benefits that come with life in one of the great cities of the world. To open Berlin still further to all Europe, East and West, let us expand the vital air access to this city, finding ways of making commercial air service to Berlin more convenient, more comfortable, and more economical. We look to the day when West Berlin can become one of the chief aviation hubs in all central Europe. With our French and British partners, the United States is prepared to help bring international meetings to Berlin.

It would be only fitting for Berlin to serve as the site of United Nations meetings, or world conferences on human rights and arms control or other issues that call for international cooperation. There is no better way to establish hope for the future than to enlighten young minds, and we would be honored to sponsor summer youth exchanges, cultural events, and other programs for young Berliners from the East. Our French and British friends, I'm certain, will do the same. And it's my hope that an authority can be found in East Berlin to sponsor visits from young people of the Western sectors.

One final proposal, one close to my heart: sport represents a source of enjoyment and ennoblement, and you many have noted that the Republic of Korea—South Korea—has offered to permit certain events of the 1988 Olympics to take place in the North. International sports competitions of all kinds could take place in both parts of this city. And what better way to demonstrate to the world the openness of this city than to offer in some future year to hold the Olympic games here in Berlin, East and West? In these four decades, as I have said, you Berliners have built a great city. You've done so in spite of threats—the Soviet attempts to impose the East mark, the blockade. Today the city thrives in spite of the challenges implicit in the very presence of this wall. What keeps you here? Certainly there's a great deal to be said for your fortitude, for your defiant courage.

But I believe there's something deeper, something that involves Berlin's whole look and feel and way of life—not mere sentiment. No one could live long in Berlin without being completely disabused of illusions. Something instead, that has seen the difficulties of life in Berlin but chose to accept them, that continues to build this good and proud city in contrast to a surrounding totalitarian presence that refuses to release human energies or aspirations. Something that speaks with a powerful voice of affirmation, that says yes to this city, yes to the future, yes to freedom.

In a word, I would submit that what keeps you in Berlin is love—love both profound and abiding. Perhaps this gets to the root of the matter, to the most fundamental distinction of all between East and West. The totalitarian world produces backwardness because it does such violence to the spirit, thwarting the human impulse to create, to enjoy, to worship. The totalitarian world finds even symbols of love and of worship an affront. Years ago, before the East Germans began rebuilding their churches, they erected a secular structure: the television tower at Alexander Platz. Virtually ever since, the authorities have been working to correct what they view as the tower's one major flaw, treating the glass sphere at the top with paints and chemicals of every kind. Yet even today when the sun strikes that sphere—that sphere that towers over all Berlin— the light makes the sign of the cross. There in Berlin, like the city itself, symbols of love, symbols of worship, cannot be suppressed. As I looked out a moment ago from the Reichstag, that embodiment of German unity, I noticed words crudely spray-painted upon the wall, perhaps by a young Berliner, "This wall will fall. Beliefs become reality." Yes, across Europe, this wall will fall. For it cannot withstand faith; it cannot withstand truth. The wall cannot withstand freedom. And I would like, before I close, to say one word. I have read, and I have been questioned since I've been here about certain demonstrations against my coming.

And I would like to say just one thing, and to those who demonstrate so. I wonder if they have ever asked themselves that if they should have the kind of government they apparently seek, no one would ever be able to do what they're doing again. Thank you and God bless you all. [174]

"Reagan's Leadership, America's Recovery"

Margaret Thatcher
National Review
December 30, 1988

There have not been many times when a British Prime Minister has been Prime Minister through two consecutive terms of office of the same President of the United States. Indeed, there have been only three such cases so far. One was Pitt the Younger, who was in Number 10 Downing Street while George Washington was President. Another was Lord Liverpool, who held the prime ministership throughout the whole period in office of President James Monroe. And I am the third. It gives me a vantage point which, if not unique, is nonetheless historically privileged from which to survey the remarkable Presidency of Ronald Reagan.

I cannot pretend, however, to be an entirely unbiased observer. I still remember vividly the feelings with which I learned of the President's election in 1980. We had met and discussed our political views some years before, when he was still Governor of California, and I knew that we believed in so many of the same things. I felt then that together we could tackle the

[174] https://www.reaganfoundation.org/media/50908/remarks_on_east_west_relations_at_brandenburg-gate_061287.pdf

formidable tasks before us: to get our countries on their feet, to restore their pride and their values, and to help create a safer and a better world.

On entering office, the President faced high interest rates, high inflation, sluggish growth, and a growing demand for self-destructive protectionism. These problems had created—and in turn were reinforced by—a feeling that not much could be done about them, that America faced inevitable decline in a new era of limits to growth, that the American dream was over. We in Britain had been in the grip of a similar pessimism during the Seventies, when political debate revolved around the concept of the "British disease." Indeed, during this entire period, the Western world seemed to be taking its temperature with every set of economic indices.

President Reagan saw instinctively that pessimism itself was the disease and that the cure for pessimism is optimism. He set about restoring faith in the prospects of the American dream—a dream of boundless opportunity built on enterprise, individual effort, and personal generosity. He infused his own belief in America's economic future in the American people. That was farsighted. It carried America through the difficult early days of the 1981–82 recession, because people are prepared to put up with sacrifices if they know that those sacrifices are the foundations of future prosperity.

Having restored the faith of the American people in themselves, the President set about liberating their energies and enterprise. He reduced the excessive burden of regulation, halted inflation, and first cut and, later, radically reformed taxation. When barriers to enterprise are removed and taxes cut to sensible levels (as we have found in Britain in recent years), people have the incentive to work harder and earn more. They thereby benefit themselves, their families, and the whole community. Hence the buoyant economy of the Reagan years. It has expanded by a full 25 per cent over 72 months of continuous economic growth—the longest period of peacetime economic growth—the longest period of peacetime economic growth in U.S. history; it has spread prosperity widely; and it has cut unemployment to the lowest level in over a decade.

The International Impact of these successes has been enormous. At a succession of Western economic summits, the President's leadership encouraged the West to cooperate on policies of low inflation, steady growth, and open markets. These policies have kept protectionism in check and the world economy growing. They are policies which offer not just an economic message, but a political one: Freedom works. It brings growth, opportunity, and prosperity in its train. Other countries, seeing its success in the United States and Britain, have rushed to adopt the policies of freedom.

President Reagan decided what he believed in, stuck to it through thick and thin, and finally, through its success, persuaded others. But I still recall those dark early days of this decade when both our countries were grappling with the twin disasters of inflation and recession and when some people, even in our own parties, wanted to abandon our policies before they had had a proper chance to take effect. They were times for cool courage and a steady nerve. That is what they got from the President. I remember his telling me, at the British Embassy in 1981, that for all the difficulties we then faced, we would be "home safe and soon enough."

The economic recovery was, however, but part of a wider recovery of America's confidence and role in the world. For the malaise of the 1970s went beyond economics. The experience of Vietnam had bred an understandable but dangerous lack of national self-confidence on the U.S. side of the Atlantic. Or so it seemed to outsiders. There was a marked reluctance in American public opinion to advance American power abroad even in defense of clear American and Western interests. And politicians struggled against this national mood at their electoral peril.

President Reagan took office at a time when the Soviet Union was invading Afghanistan, placing missiles in Eastern Europe aimed at West European capitals, and assisting Communist groups in the Third World to install themselves in power against the popular will, and when America's response was hobbled by the so-called "Vietnam syndrome." And not just America's response. The entire West, locked in a battle of wills with the Soviets, seemed to be losing confidence.

President Reagan's first step was to change the military imbalance which underlay this loss of confidence. He built up American power in a series of defense budgets. There have been criticisms of this build-up as too expensive. Well, a sure defense *is* expensive, but not nearly so expensive as weakness could turn out to be.

By this military build-up, President Reagan strengthened not only American defenses, but also the will of America's allies. It led directly to NATO's installation of cruise and Pershing missiles in Western Europe. This took place in the teeth of Moscow's biggest "peace offensive" since the Berlin crises of the early Sixties. That offensive included a Soviet walkout from the Geneva talks on nuclear disarmament and mass demonstrations and lobbies by "peace groups" in Western Europe. Yet these tactics failed, the missiles were installed, and the Soviets returned to the bargaining table to negotiate about withdrawing their own missiles.

President Reagan has also demonstrated that he is not afraid to put to good use the military strength he had built up. And it is noteworthy—though not often noted—that many of the decisions he has taken in the face of strong criticism have been justified by events. It was President Reagan who, amid cries that his policy lacked any rationale, stationed U.S. ships alongside European navies in the Persian Gulf to protect international shipping. Not only did this policy secure its stated purpose, it also protected the Gulf states against aggression and thus hastened the end of the conflict by foreclosing any option of widening the war.

The President enjoyed a similar success in the continuing battle against terrorism. He took action against one of the states most active in giving aid and comfort to terrorist organizations: Colonel Qaddafi's Libya. We in Britain had experienced Qaddafi's murderous methods at first hand when a member of the Libyan Embassy shot down a young policewoman in cold blood in a London square. We had no doubts about the reality of Libyan involvement. I therefore had no hesitation in supporting the American air strike, which has resulted in a marked reduction of Libyan-sponsored terrorism.

And, thirdly, President Reagan has given America's support to nations which are still struggling to keep their independence in the face of Soviet-backed aggression. The policy has had major successes:

— the withdrawal of Soviet forces from Afghanistan, due to be completed next February;

— the real prospect of Cuban withdrawal from Angola, encouraged by patient and constructive American diplomacy;

— and even the prospect of Vietnamese withdrawal from Cambodia.

These are all remarkable achievements, which very few observers predicted even three years ago.

Indeed, when we compare the mood of confidence and optimism in the West today with the mood when President Reagan took office eight years ago, we know that a greater change has taken place than could ever have been imagined. America has regained its confidence and is no longer afraid of the legitimate uses of its power. It has discussed those uses with its allies in the NATO alliance at all stages and with great frankness. Today our joint resolve is stronger than ever. And, finally, the recovery of American strength and confidence has led, as President Reagan always argued it would, to more peaceful and stable relations with the Soviet Union.

For strength, not weakness, leads to peace. It was only after the Soviet threat of SS-20s had been faced down and cruise and Pershing missiles installed that the Soviets were prepared to embark on genuine arms-control negotiations and wider peace negotiations. It therefore fell to the President, less than four years after the Soviet walkout at Geneva, to negotiate the first arms-control agreement that actually reduced the nuclear stockpiles. And when he visited Moscow for the third Summit of his Presidency, he took the fight for human rights into the very heart of Moscow, where his words shone like a beacon of hope for all those who are denied their basic freedoms. Indeed the very recovery of American strength during his Presidency has been a major factor prompting and evoking the reform program under Mr. Gorbachev in the Soviet Union. The Soviet authorities would have had much less incentive for reform if they had been faced by a weak and declining United States.

The legacy of President Reagan in East-West relations is the realistic appreciation that maintaining sure defenses, bridging the East-West divide, and reducing weapons and forces on both sides are not contradictory but policies that go comfortably together. Nothing could be more short-sighted for the West today than to run down its defenses unilaterally at the first sign of more peaceful and stable relations between East and West. Nothing would be more likely to convince those with whom we negotiate that they would not need to make any concessions because we would cut our defenses anyway. Britain will not do that. We will maintain and update our defenses. And our example is one which I hope our partners and allies will follow, because Europe must show that she is willing to bear a reasonable share of the burden of defending herself. That would be the best way for the NATO allies to repay America's farsighted foreign and defense policies of the Reagan years.

When we attempt an overall survey of President Reagan's term of office, covering events both foreign and domestic, one thing stands out. It is that he has achieved the most difficult of all political tasks: changing attitudes and perceptions about what is possible. From the strong fortress of his convictions, he set out to enlarge freedom the world over at a time when freedom was in retreat—and he succeeded. It is not merely that freedom now advances while collectivism is in retreat—important though that is. It is that freedom is the idea that everywhere captures men's minds while collectivism can do no more than enslave their bodies. That is the measure of the change that President Reagan has wrought.

How is it that some political leaders make the world a different place while others, equally able, equally public-spirited, leave things much as they found them? Some years ago, Professor Hayek pointed out that the social sciences often neglected the most important aspects of their subjects because they were not capable of being examined and explained in quantitative terms. One such quality which resists quantitative analysis is political leadership. Which also happens to be the occupational requirement of a statesman.

No one can doubt that President Reagan possesses the ability to lead to an unusual degree. Some of the constituent qualities of that leadership I have referred to in passing—his firm convictions, his steadfastness in difficult times, his capacity to infuse his own optimism into the American people so that he restored their belief in America's destiny. But I would add three more qualities that, together with those above, enabled him to transform the political landscape.

The first is courage. The whole world remembers the wit and grace which the President displayed at the time of the attempt on his life. It was one of those occasions when people saw the real character of a man when he had none of the assistances which power and office provide. And they admired what they saw—cheerful bravery in the face of personal danger, no thought for himself but instead a desire to reassure his family and the nation by jokes and good humor.

The second is that he holds opinions which strike a chord in the heart of the average American. The great English journalist

Walter Bagehot once defined a constitutional statesman as a man of common opinion and uncommon abilities. That is true of President Reagan and one of his greatest political strengths. He can appeal for support to the American people because they sense rightly that he shares their dreams, hopes, and aspirations; and he pursues them by the same route of plain American horse-sense.

Finally, President Reagan speaks with the authority of a man who knows what he believes and who has shown that he will stand by his beliefs in good times and bad. He is no summer soldier of conservatism, but one who fought in the ranks when the going wasn't good. Again, that reassures even those who do not share those beliefs. For authority is the respect won from others by the calm exercise of deep conviction.

The results of that leadership are all around us. President Reagan departs the political scene leaving America stronger and more confident, and the West more united, than ever before. I believe that President-elect Bush, a man of unrivaled experience in government and international affairs, will be a worthy successor, providing the forthright leadership which the world has come to expect from the U.S. President. We wish him well.[175]

President Ronald Reagan's Proclamation 5599—National Sanctity of Human Life Day

January 16, 1987

In 1973, America's unborn children lost their legal protection. In the 14 years since then, some twenty million unborn babies, 1.5

---

[175]   https://www.margaretthatcher.org/document/107425

million each year, have lost their lives by abortion—in a nation of 242 million people. This tragic and terrible toll continues, at the rate of more than 4,000 young lives lost each day. This is a shameful record; it accords with neither human decency nor our American heritage of respect for the sanctity of human life.

That heritage is deeply rooted in the hearts and the history of our people. Our Founding Fathers pledged to each other their lives, their fortunes, and their sacred honor in the Declaration of Independence. They announced their unbreakable bonds with its immutable truths that "all men are created equal, that they are endowed by their Creator with certain unalienable Rights, that among these are Life, Liberty and the pursuit of Happiness." Americans of every succeeding generation have cherished our heritage of God-given human rights and have been willing to sacrifice for those rights, just as our Founders did.

Those rights are given by God to all alike. Medical evidence leaves no room for doubt that the distinct being developing in a mother's womb is both alive and human. This merely confirms what common sense has always told us. Abortion kills unborn babies and denies them forever their rights to "Life, Liberty and the pursuit of Happiness." Our Declaration of Independence holds that governments are instituted among men to secure these rights, and our Constitution—founded on these principles—should not be read to sanction the taking of innocent human life.

A return to our heritage of reverence and protection for the sanctity of innocent human life is long overdue. For the last 14 years and longer, many Americans have devoted themselves to restoring the right to life and to providing loving alternatives to abortion so every mother will choose life for her baby.

We must recognize the courage and love mothers exhibit in keeping their babies or choosing adoption. We must also offer thanks and support to the millions of Americans who are willing to take on the responsibilities of adoptive parents. And we must never cease our efforts—our appeals to the legislatures and the courts and our prayers to the Author of Life Himself—until infants before birth are once again afforded the same protection of the law we all enjoy.

Our heritage as Americans bids us to respect and to defend the sanctity of human life. With every confidence in the blessing of God and the goodness of the American people, let us rededicate ourselves to this solemn duty.

Now, Therefore, I, Ronald Reagan, President of the United States of America, by virtue of the authority vested in me by the Constitution and laws of the United States, do hereby proclaim Sunday, January 18, 1987, as National Sanctity of Human Life Day. I call upon the citizens of this blessed land to gather on that day in homes and places of worship to give thanks for the gift of life and to reaffirm our commitment to the dignity of every human being and the sanctity of each human life.

In Witness Whereof, I have hereunto set my hand this 16th day of January, in the year of our Lord nineteen hundred and eighty-seven, and of the Independence of the United States of America the two hundred and eleventh.[176]

"The Flight 93 Election"

---

[176] https://www.sba-list.org/suzy-b-blog/president-reagans-legacy-life

Publius Decius Mus (Michael Anton)
This essay first ran in the Claremont Review of Books,
September 5, 2016.

2016 is the Flight 93 election: charge the cockpit or you die. You
may die anyway. You—or the leader of your party—may make
it into the cockpit and not know how to fly or land the plane.
There are no guarantees.

Except one: if you don't try, death is certain. To compound
the metaphor: a Hillary Clinton presidency is Russian Roulette
with a semi-auto. With Trump, at least you can spin the cylin-
der and take your chances.

To ordinary conservative ears, this sounds histrionic. The
stakes can't be that high because they are never that high—except
perhaps in the pages of Gibbon. Conservative intellectuals will
insist that there has been no "end of history" and that all human
outcomes are still possible. They will even—as Charles Kesler
does—admit that America is in "crisis." But how great is the
crisis? Can things really be so bad if eight years of Obama can
be followed by eight more of Hillary, and yet Constitutionalist
conservatives can still reasonably hope for a restoration of our
cherished ideals? Cruz in 2024!

Not to pick (too much) on Kesler, who is less unwarrantedly
optimistic than most conservatives. And who, at least, poses
the right question: Trump or Hillary? Though his answer—
"even if [Trump] had chosen his policies at random, they would
be sounder than Hillary's"—is unwarrantedly ungenerous. The
truth is that Trump articulated, if incompletely and inconsis-
tently, the right stances on the right issues—immigration, trade,
and war—right from the beginning.

But let us back up. One of the paradoxes—there are so many—of conservative thought over the last decade at least is the unwillingness even to *entertain* the possibility that America and the West are on a trajectory toward something very bad. On the one hand, conservatives routinely present a litany of ills plaguing the body politic. Illegitimacy. Crime. Massive, expensive, intrusive, out-of-control government. Politically correct McCarthyism. Ever-higher taxes and ever-deteriorating services and infrastructure. Inability to win wars against tribal, sub-Third-World foes. A disastrously awful educational system that churns out kids who don't know anything and, at the primary and secondary levels, can't (or won't) discipline disruptive punks, and at the higher levels saddles students with six figure debts for the privilege. And so on and drearily on. Like that portion of the mass where the priest asks for your private intentions, fill in any dismal fact about American decline that you want and I'll stipulate it.

Conservatives spend at least several hundred million dollars a year on think-tanks, magazines, conferences, fellowships, and such, complaining about this, that, the other, and everything. And yet these same conservatives are, at root, keepers of the *status quo*. Oh, sure, they want some things to change. They want their pet ideas adopted—tax deductions for having more babies and the like. Many of them are even good ideas. But are any of them truly fundamental? Do they get to the heart of our problems?

If conservatives are right about the importance of virtue, morality, religious faith, stability, character and so on in the individual; if they are right about sexual morality or what came to be termed "family values"; if they are right about the importance of education to inculcate good character and to teach the fundamentals that have defined knowledge in the West for millennia; if they are right about societal norms and public order; if they are right about the centrality of initiative, enterprise, industry, and thrift to a sound economy and a healthy society; if they are right about the soul-sapping effects of paternalistic Big Government and its cannibalization of civil society and religious institutions; if they are right about the necessity of a strong defense and prudent statesmanship in the international sphere—if they are right about the importance of all this to national health and even survival, then they must believe—mustn't they?—that *we are headed off a cliff*.

But it's quite obvious that conservatives don't believe any such thing, that they feel no such sense of urgency, of an immediate necessity to change course and avoid the cliff. A recent article by Matthew Continetti may be taken as representative—indeed, almost written for the purpose of illustrating the point. Continetti inquires into the "condition of America" and finds it wanting. What does Continetti propose to do about it? The usual litany of "conservative" "solutions," with the obligatory references to decentralization, federalization, "civic renewal," and—of course!—Burke. Which is to say, conservatism's typical combination of the useless and inapt with the utopian and unrealizable. Decentralization and federalism are all well and good, and as a conservative, I endorse them both without reservation. But how are they going to save, or even meaningfully improve, the America that Continetti describes? What can they do against a tidal wave of dysfunction, immorality, and corruption? "Civic renewal" would do a lot of course, but that's like saying health will save a cancer patient. A step has been skipped in there somewhere. How are we going to *achieve* "civic renewal"? Wishing for a tautology to enact itself is not a strategy.

Continetti trips over a more promising approach when he writes of "stress[ing] the 'national interest abroad and national solidarity at home' through foreign-policy retrenchment, 'support to workers buffeted by globalization,' and setting 'tax rates and immigration levels' to foster social cohesion." That sounds a lot like Trumpism. But the phrases that Continetti quotes are taken from Ross Douthat and Reihan Salam, both of whom, like Continetti, are vociferously—one might even say fanatically—anti-Trump. At least they, unlike Kesler, give Trump credit for having identified the right stance on today's most salient issues. Yet, paradoxically, they won't vote for Trump whereas Kesler hints that he will. It's reasonable, then, to read into Kesler's esoteric endorsement of Trump an implicit acknowledgment that the crisis is, indeed, pretty dire. I expect a Claremont scholar to be wiser than most other conservative intellectuals, and I am relieved not to be disappointed in this instance.

Yet we may also reasonably ask: What explains the Pollyanna-ish declinism of so many others? That is, the stance that Things-Are-Really-Bad—But-Not-So-Bad-that-We-Have-to-Consider-Anything-Really-Different! The obvious answer is that they don't really believe the first half of that formulation. If so, like Chicken Little, they should stick a sock in it. Pecuniary reasons also suggest themselves, but let us foreswear recourse to this explanation until we have disproved all the others.

Whatever the reason for the contradiction, there can be no doubt that there *is* a contradiction. To simultaneously hold conservative cultural, economic, and political beliefs—to insist that our liberal-left present reality and future direction is incompatible with human nature and must undermine society—and yet also believe that things can go on more or less the way they are going, ideally but not necessarily with some conservative tinkering here and there, is logically impossible.

Let's be very blunt here: if you genuinely think things can go on with no fundamental change needed, then you have implicitly admitted that *conservatism is wrong*. Wrong philosophically, wrong on human nature, wrong on the nature of politics, and wrong in its policy prescriptions. Because, first, few of those prescriptions are in force today. Second, of the ones that are, the left is busy undoing them, often with conservative assistance. And, third, the whole trend of the West is ever-leftward, ever further away from what we all understand as conservatism.

If your answer—Continetti's, Douthat's, Salam's, and so many others'—is for conservatism to keep doing what it's been doing—another policy journal, another article about welfare reform, another half-day seminar on limited government, another tax credit proposal—even though we've been losing ground for at least a century, then you've implicitly accepted that your supposed political philosophy doesn't matter and that civilization will carry on just fine under leftist tenets. Indeed, that leftism is *truer* than conservatism and superior to it.

They will say, in words reminiscent of dorm-room Marxism—but our proposals have *not* been tried! Here our ideas sit, waiting to be implemented! To which I reply: eh, not really. Many conservative solutions—above all welfare reform and crime control—*have* been tried, and proved effective, but have nonetheless failed to stem the tide. Crime, for instance, is down from its mid-'70s and early '90s peak—but way, way up from the historic American norm that ended when liberals took over criminal justice in the mid-'60s. And it's rising fast today, in the teeth of ineffectual conservative complaints. And what has this temporary crime (or welfare, for that matter) decline done to stem the greater tide? The tsunami of leftism that still engulfs our every—literal and figurative—shore has receded not a bit but indeed has grown. All your (our) victories are short-lived.

More to the point, what has conservatism achieved *lately*? In the last 20 years? The answer—which appears to be "nothing"—might seem to lend credence to the plea that "our ideas haven't been tried." Except that the same conservatives who generate those ideas are in charge of selling them to the broader public. If their ideas "haven't been tried," who is ultimately at fault? The whole enterprise of Conservatism, Inc., reeks of failure. Its sole recent and ongoing success is its own self-preservation. Conservative intellectuals never tire of praising "entrepreneurs" and "creative destruction." Dare to fail! they exhort businessmen. Let the market decide! Except, um, not with respect to us. Or is their true market not the political arena, but the fundraising circuit?

Only three questions matter. First, how bad are things really? Second, what do we do right now? Third, what should we do for the long term?

Conservatism, Inc.'s, "answer" to the first may, at this point, simply be dismissed. If the conservatives wish to have a serious debate, I for one am game—more than game; eager. The problem of "subjective certainty" can only be overcome by going into the agora. But my attempt to do so—the blog that Kesler mentions—was met largely with incredulity. How can they say that?! How can anyone apparently of our caste (conservative intellectuals) not merely *support* Trump (however lukewarmly) but offer *reasons* for doing do?

One of the *Journal of American Greatness*'s deeper arguments was that only in a corrupt republic, in corrupt times, could a Trump rise. It is therefore puzzling that those most horrified by Trump are the least willing to consider the possibility that the republic is dying. That possibility, apparently, seems to them so preposterous that no refutation is necessary.

As does, presumably, the argument that the stakes in 2016 are—everything. I should here note that I am a good deal gloomier than my (former) *JAG* colleagues, and that while we frequently used the royal "we" when discussing things on which we all agreed, I here speak only for myself.

How have the last two decades worked out for you, personally? If you're a member or fellow-traveler of the Davos class, chances are: pretty well. If you're among the subspecies conservative intellectual or politician, you've accepted—perhaps not consciously, but unmistakably—your status on the roster of the Washington Generals of American politics. Your job is to show up and lose, but you are a necessary part of the show and you do get paid. To the extent that you are ever on the winning side of anything, it's as sophists who help the Davoisie oligarchy rationalize open borders, lower wages, outsourcing, de-industrialization, trade giveaways, and endless, pointless, winless war.

All of Trump's 16 Republican competitors would have ensured more of the same—as will the election of Hillary Clinton. That would be bad enough. But at least Republicans are merely reactive when it comes to wholesale cultural and political change. Their "opposition" may be in all cases ineffectual and often indistinguishable from support. But they don't dream up inanities like 32 "genders," elective bathrooms, single-payer, Iran sycophancy, "Islamophobia," and Black Lives Matter. They merely help ratify them.

A Hillary presidency will be pedal-to-the-metal on the entire Progressive-left agenda, plus items few of us have yet imagined in our darkest moments. Nor is even that the worst. It will be coupled with a level of vindictive persecution against resistance and dissent hitherto seen in the supposedly liberal West only in the most "advanced" Scandinavian countries and the most leftist corners of Germany and England. We see this already in the censorship practiced by the Davoisie's social media enablers; in the shameless propaganda tidal wave of the mainstream media; and in the personal destruction campaigns—operated through the former and aided by the latter—of the Social Justice Warriors. We see it in Obama's flagrant use of the IRS to torment political opponents, the gaslighting denial by the media, and the collective shrug by everyone else.

It's absurd to assume that any of this would stop or slow—would do anything other than massively intensify—in a Hillary administration. It's even more ridiculous to expect that hitherto useless conservative opposition would suddenly become effective. For two generations at least, the Left has been calling everyone to their right Nazis. This trend has accelerated exponentially in the last few years, helped along by some on the Right who really do seem to merit—and even relish—the label. There is nothing the modern conservative fears more than being called "racist," so alt-right pocket Nazis are manna from heaven for the Left. But also wholly unnecessary: sauce for the goose. The Left was calling us Nazis long before any pro-Trumpers tweeted Holocaust denial memes. And how does one deal with a Nazi—that is, with an enemy one is convinced intends your destruction? You don't compromise with him or leave him alone. You crush him.

So what do we have to lose by fighting back? Only our Washington Generals jerseys—and paychecks. But those are going away anyway. Among the many things the "Right" still doesn't understand is that the Left has concluded that this particular show need no longer go on. They don't think they need a foil anymore and would rather dispense with the whole bother of staging these phony contests in which each side ostensibly has a shot.

If you haven't noticed, our side has been losing consistently since 1988. We can win midterms, but we do nothing with them. Call ours Hannibalic victories. After the Carthaginian's famous slaughter of a Roman army at Cannae, he failed to march on an undefended Rome, prompting his cavalry commander to complain: "you know how to win a victory, but not how to use one." And, aside from 2004's lackluster 50.7%, we can't win the big ones at all.

Because the deck is stacked overwhelmingly against us. I will mention but three ways. First, the opinion-making elements—the universities and the media above all—are wholly corrupt and wholly opposed to everything we want, and increasingly even to our existence. (What else are the wars on "cis-genderism"—formerly known as "nature"—and on the supposed "white privilege" of broke hillbillies really about?) If it hadn't been abundantly clear for the last 50 years, the campaign of 2015-2016 must surely have made it evident to even the meanest capacities that the intelligentsia—including all the organs through which it broadcasts its propaganda—is overwhelmingly partisan and biased. Against this onslaught, "conservative" media is a nullity, barely a whisper. It cannot be heard above the blaring of what has been aptly called "The Megaphone."

Second, our Washington Generals self-handicap and self-censor to an absurd degree. Lenin is supposed to have said that "the best way to control the opposition is to lead it ourselves." But with an opposition like ours, why bother? Our "leaders" and "dissenters" bend over backward to play by the self-sabotaging rules the Left sets for them. Fearful, beaten dogs have more *thymos*.

Third and most important, the ceaseless importation of Third World foreigners with no tradition of, taste for, or experience in liberty means that the electorate grows more left, more Democratic, less Republican, less republican, and less traditionally American with every cycle. As does, of course, the U.S. population, which only serves to reinforce the two other causes outlined above. This is the core reason why the Left, the Democrats, and the bipartisan junta (categories distinct but very much overlapping) think they are on the cusp of a permanent victory that will forever obviate the need to pretend to respect democratic and constitutional niceties. Because they are.

It's also why they treat open borders as the "absolute value," the one "principle" that—when their "principles" collide—they prioritize above all the others. If *that* fact is insufficiently clear, consider this. Trump is the most liberal Republican nominee since Thomas Dewey. He departs from conservative orthodoxy in so many ways that *National Review* still hasn't stopped counting. But let's stick to just the core issues animating his campaign. On trade, globalization, and war, Trump is to the left (conventionally understood) not only of his own party, but of his Democratic opponent. And yet the Left and the junta are at one with the house-broken conservatives in their determination—desperation—not merely to defeat Trump but to destroy him. What gives?

Oh, right—there's that *other* issue. The sacredness of mass immigration is the mystic chord that unites America's ruling and intellectual classes. Their reasons vary somewhat. The Left and the Democrats seek ringers to form a permanent electoral majority. They, or many of them, also believe the academic-intellectual lie that America's inherently racist and evil nature can be expiated only through ever greater "diversity." The junta of course craves cheaper and more docile labor. It also seeks to legitimize, and deflect unwanted attention from, its wealth and power by pretending that its open borders stance is a form of *noblesse oblige*. The Republicans and the "conservatives"? Both of course desperately want absolution from the charge of "racism." For the latter, this at least makes some sense. No Washington General can take the court—much less cash his check—with that epithet dancing over his head like some Satanic Spirit. But for the former, this priestly grace comes at the direct expense of their worldly interests. Do they honestly believe that the right enterprise zone or charter school policy will arouse 50.01% of our newer voters to finally reveal their "natural conservatism" at the ballot box? It hasn't happened anywhere yet and shows no signs that it ever will. But that doesn't stop the Republican refrain: more, more, more! No matter how many elections they lose, how many districts tip forever blue, how rarely (if ever) their immigrant vote cracks 40%, the answer is always the same. Just like Angela Merkel after yet another rape, shooting, bombing, or machete attack. More, more, more!

This is insane. This is the mark of a party, a society, a country, a people, a civilization that wants to die. Trump, alone among candidates for high office in this or in the last seven (at least) cycles, has stood up to say: I want to live. I want my party to live. I want my country to live. I want my people to live. I want to end the insanity.

Yes, Trump is worse than imperfect. So what? We can lament until we choke the lack of a great statesman to address the fundamental issues of our time—or, more importantly, to connect them. Since Pat Buchanan's three failures, occasionally a candidate arose who saw one piece: Dick Gephardt on trade, Ron Paul on war, Tom Tancredo on immigration. Yet, among recent political figures—great statesmen, dangerous demagogues, and mewling gnats alike—only Trump-the-alleged-buffoon not merely saw all three and their essential connectivity, *but was able to win on them*. The alleged buffoon is thus more prudent— more practically wise—than all of our wise-and-good who so bitterly oppose him. This should embarrass them. That their failures instead embolden them is only further proof of their foolishness and hubris.

Which they self-laud as "consistency"—adherence to "conservative principle," defined by the 1980 campaign and the household gods of reigning conservative think-tanks. A higher consistency in the service of the national interest apparently eludes them. When America possessed a vast, empty continent and explosively growing industry, high immigration was arguably good policy. (*Arguably*: Ben Franklin would disagree.) It hasn't made sense since World War I. Free trade was unquestionably a great boon to the American worker in the decades after World War II. We long ago passed the point of diminishing returns. The Gulf War of 1991 was a strategic victory for American interests. No conflict since then has been. Conservatives either can't see this—or, worse, those who can nonetheless treat the only political leader to mount a serious challenge to the status quo (more immigration, more trade, more war) as a unique evil.

Trump's vulgarity is in fact a godsend to the conservatives. It allows them to hang their public opposition on his obvious shortcomings and to ignore or downplay his far greater strengths, which should be even more obvious but in corrupt times can be deliberately obscured by constant references to his faults. That the Left would make the campaign all about the latter is to be expected. Why would the Right? Some—a few— are no doubt sincere in their belief that the man is simply unfit for high office. David Frum, who has always been an immigration skeptic and is a convert to the less-war position, is sincere when he says that, even though he agrees with much of Trump's agenda, he cannot stomach Trump. But for most of the other #NeverTrumpers, is it just a coincidence that they also happen to favor Invade the World, Invite the World?

Another question *JAG* raised without provoking any serious attempt at refutation was whether, in corrupt times, it took a…let's say…"loudmouth" to rise above the din of The Megaphone. We, or I, speculated: "yes." Suppose there had arisen some statesman of high character—dignified, articulate, experienced, knowledgeable—the exact opposite of everything the conservatives claim to hate about Trump. Could this hypothetical paragon have won on Trump's same issues? Would the conservatives have supported him? I would have—even had he been a Democrat.

Back on planet earth, that flight of fancy at least addresses what to do now. The answer to the subsidiary question—will it work?—is much less clear. By "it" I mean Trumpism, broadly defined as secure borders, economic nationalism, and America-first foreign policy. We Americans have chosen, in our foolishness, to disunite the country through stupid immigration, economic, and foreign policies. The level of unity America enjoyed before the bipartisan junta took over can never be restored.

But we can probably do better than we are doing now. First, stop digging. No more importing poverty, crime, and alien cultures. We have made institutions, by leftist design, not merely abysmal at assimilation but abhorrent of the concept. We should try to fix that, but given the Left's iron grip on every school and cultural center, that's like trying to bring democracy to Russia. A worthy goal, perhaps, but temper your hopes—and don't invest time and resources unrealistically.

By contrast, simply building a wall and enforcing immigration law will help enormously, by cutting off the flood of newcomers that perpetuates ethnic separatism and by incentivizing the English language and American norms in the workplace. These policies will have the added benefit of aligning the economic interests of, and (we may hope) fostering solidarity among, the working, lower middle, and middle classes of all races and ethnicities. The same can be said for Trumpian trade policies and anti-globalization instincts. Who cares if productivity numbers tick down, or if our already somnambulant GDP sinks a bit further into its pillow? Nearly all the gains of the last 20 years have accrued to the junta anyway. It would, at this point, be better for the nation to divide up more equitably a slightly smaller pie than to add one extra slice—only to ensure that it and eight of the other nine go first to the government and its rentiers, and the rest to the same four industries and 200 families.

Will this work? Ask a pessimist, get a pessimistic answer. So don't ask. Ask instead: is it worth trying? Is it better than the alternative? If you can't say, forthrightly, "yes," you are either part of the junta, a fool, or a conservative intellectual.

And if it doesn't work, what then? We've established that most "conservative" anti-Trumpites are in the Orwellian sense objectively pro-Hillary. What about the rest of you? If you recognize the threat she poses, but somehow can't stomach him, have you thought about the longer term? The possibilities would seem to be: Caesarism, secession/crack-up, collapse, or managerial Davoisie liberalism as far as the eye can see...which, since nothing human lasts forever, at some point will give way to one of the other three. Oh, and, I suppose, for those who like to pour a tall one and dream big, a second American Revolution that restores Constitutionalism, limited government, and a 28% top marginal rate.

But for those of you who are sober: can you sketch a more plausible long-term future than the prior four following a Trump defeat? I can't either.

The election of 2016 is a test—in my view, the final test—of whether there is any *virtù* left in what used to be the core of the American nation. If they cannot rouse themselves simply to *vote* for the first candidate in a generation who pledges to advance their interests, and to vote *against* the one who openly boasts that she will do the opposite (a million more Syrians, anyone?), then they are doomed. They may not deserve the fate that will befall them, but they will suffer it regardless.[177]

President Ronald Reagan's Second Inaugural Speech

January 21, 1985
Remarks as prepared for delivery.

Senator Mathias, Chief Justice Burger, Vice President Bush, Speaker O'Neill, Senator Dole, Reverend Clergy, members of my family and friends, and my fellow citizens:

This day has been made brighter with the presence here of one who, for a time, has been absent—Senator John Stennis.

God bless you and welcome back.

There is, however, one who is not with us today: Representative Gillis Long of Louisiana left us last night. I wonder if we could all join in a moment of silent prayer. Amen.

There are no words adequate to express my thanks for the great honor that you have bestowed on me. I will do my utmost to be deserving of your trust.

This is, as Senator Mathias told us, the fiftieth time that we the people have celebrated this historic occasion. When the first president, George Washington, placed his hand upon the Bible, he stood less than a single day's journey by horseback from raw, untamed wilderness. There were four million Americans in a union of thirteen States. Today we are sixty times as many in a union of fifty states. We have lighted the world with our inventions, gone to the aid of mankind wherever in the world there was a cry for help, journeyed to the moon and safely returned. So much has changed. And yet we stand together as we did two centuries ago.

When I took this oath four years ago, I did so in a time of economic stress. Voices were raised saying we had to look to our past for the greatness and glory. But we, the present-day Americans, are not given to looking backward. In this blessed land, there is always a better tomorrow.

Four years ago, I spoke to you of a new beginning, and we have accomplished that. But in another sense, our new beginning is a continuation of that beginning created two centuries ago when, for the first time in history, government, the people said, was not our master; it is our servant, its only power that which we the people allow it to have.

That system has never failed us, but, for a time, we failed the system. We asked things of government that government was not equipped to give. We yielded authority to the national government that properly belonged to states or to local governments or to the people themselves. We allowed taxes and inflation to rob us of our earnings and savings and watched the great industrial machine that had made us the most productive people on Earth slow down and the number of unemployed increase.

By 1980, we knew it was time to renew our faith, to strive with all our strength toward the ultimate in individual freedom consistent with an orderly society.

We believed then and now there are no limits to growth and human progress when men and women are free to follow their dreams.

And we were right to believe that. Tax rates have been reduced, inflation cut dramatically, and more people are employed than ever before in our history.

We are creating a nation once again vibrant, robust, and alive. But there are many mountains yet to climb. We will not rest until every American enjoys the fullness of freedom, dignity, and opportunity as our birthright. It is our birthright as citizens of this great republic, and we'll meet this challenge.

These will be years when Americans have restored their confidence and tradition of progress; when our values of faith, family, work, and neighborhood were restated for a modern age; when our economy was finally freed from government's grip; when we made sincere efforts at meaningful arms reduction, rebuilding our defenses, our economy, and developing new technologies, and helped preserve peace in a troubled world; when Americans courageously supported the struggle for liberty, self-government, and free enterprise throughout the world, and turned the tide of history away from totalitarian darkness and into the warm sunlight of human freedom.

My fellow citizens, our nation is poised for greatness. We must do what we know is right and do it with all our might. Let history say of us, "These were golden years—when the American Revolution was reborn, when freedom gained new life, when America reached for her best."

Our two-party system has served us well over the years, but never better than in those times of great challenge when we came together not as Democrats or Republicans, but as Americans united in a common cause.

Two of our Founding Fathers, a Boston lawyer named Adams and a Virginia planter named Jefferson, members of that remarkable group who met in Independence Hall and dared to think they could start the world over again, left us an important lesson. They had become political rivals in the presidential election of 1800. Then years later, when both were retired, and age had softened their anger, they began to speak to each other again through letters. A bond was reestablished between those two who had helped create this government of ours.

In 1826, the fiftieth anniversary of the Declaration of Independence, they both died. They died on the same day, within a few hours of each other, and that day was the Fourth of July.

In one of those letters exchanged in the sunset of their lives, Jefferson wrote: "It carries me back to the times when, beset with difficulties and dangers, we were fellow laborers in the same cause, struggling for what is most valuable to man, his right to self-government. Laboring always at the same oar, with some wave ever ahead threatening to overwhelm us, and yet passing harmless...we rode through the storm with heart and hand."

Well, with heart and hand, let us stand as one today: one people under God determined that our future shall be worthy of our past. As we do, we must not repeat the well-intentioned errors of our past. We must never again abuse the trust of working men and women, by sending their earnings on a futile chase after the spiraling demands of a bloated federal Establishment. You elected us in 1980 to end this prescription for disaster, and I don't believe you reelected us in 1984 to reverse course.

At the heart of our efforts is one idea vindicated by twenty-five straight months of economic growth: freedom and incentives unleash the drive and entrepreneurial genius that are the core of human progress. We have begun to increase the rewards for work, savings, and investment; reduce the increase in the cost and size of government and its interference in people's lives.

We must simplify our tax system, make it more fair, and bring the rates down for all who work and earn. We must think anew and move with a new boldness, so every American who seeks work can find work; so the least among us shall have an equal chance to achieve the greatest things—to be heroes who heal our sick, feed the hungry, protect peace among nations, and leave this world a better place.

The time has come for a new American emancipation—a great national drive to tear down economic barriers and liberate the spirit of enterprise in the most distressed areas of our country. My friends, together we can do this, and do it we must, so help me God. From new freedom will spring new opportunities for growth, a more productive, fulfilled and united people, and a stronger America—an America that will lead the technological revolution, and also open its mind and heart and soul to the treasures of literature, music, and poetry, and the values of faith, courage, and love.

A dynamic economy, with more citizens working and paying taxes, will be our strongest tool to bring down budget deficits. But an almost unbroken fifty years of deficit spending has finally brought us to a time of reckoning. We have come to a turning point, a moment for hard decisions. I have asked the Cabinet and my staff a question, and now I put the same question to all of you: if not us, who? And if not now, when? It must be done by all of us going forward with a program aimed at reaching a balanced budget. We can then begin reducing the national debt.

I will shortly submit a budget to the Congress aimed at freezing government program spending for the next year. Beyond that, we must take further steps to permanently control government's power to tax and spend. We must act now to protect future generations from government's desire to spend its citizens' money and tax them into servitude when the bills come due. Let us make it unconstitutional for the federal government to spend more than the federal government takes in.

We have already started returning to the people and to state and local governments responsibilities better handled by them. Now, there is a place for the federal government in matters of social compassion. But our fundamental goals must be to reduce dependency and upgrade the dignity of those who are infirm or disadvantaged. And here a growing economy and support from family and community offer our best chance for a society where compassion is a way of life, where the old and infirm are cared for, the young and, yes, the unborn protected, and the unfortunate looked after and made self

And there is another area where the federal government can play a part. As an older American, I remember a time when people of different race, creed, or ethnic origin in our land found hatred and prejudice installed in social custom and, yes, in law. There is no story more heartening in our history than the progress that we have made toward the "brotherhood of man" that God intended for us. Let us resolve there will be no turning back or hesitation on the road to an America rich in dignity and abundant with opportunity for all our citizens.

Let us resolve that we the people will build an American opportunity society in which all of us—white and black, rich and poor, young and old—will go forward together arm in arm. Again, let us remember that though our heritage is one of bloodlines from every corner of the earth, we are all Americans pledged to carry on this last, best hope of man on Earth.

I have spoken of our domestic goals and the limitations which we should put on our national government. Now let me turn to a task which is the primary responsibility of national government—the safety and security of our people.

Today, we utter no prayer more fervently than the ancient prayer for peace on Earth. Yet history has shown that peace will not come, nor will our freedom be preserved, by goodwill alone. There are those in the world who scorn our vision of human dignity and freedom. One nation, the Soviet Union, has conducted the greatest military buildup in the history of man, building arsenals of awesome offensive weapons.

We have made progress in restoring our defense capability. But much remains to be done. There must be no wavering by us, nor any doubts by others, that America will meet her responsibilities to remain free, secure, and at peace.

There is only one way safely and legitimately to reduce the cost of national security, and that is to reduce the need for it. And this we are trying to do in negotiations with the Soviet Union. We are not just discussing limits on a further increase of nuclear weapons. We seek, instead, to reduce their number. We seek the total elimination one day of nuclear weapons from the face of the earth.

Now, for decades, we and the Soviets have lived under the threat of mutual assured destruction; if either resorted to the use of nuclear weapons, the other could retaliate and destroy the one who had started it. Is there either logic or morality in believing that if one side threatens to kill tens of millions of our people, our only recourse is to threaten killing tens of millions of theirs?

I have approved a research program to find, if we can, a security shield that would destroy nuclear missiles before they reach their target. It wouldn't kill people; it would destroy weapons. It wouldn't militarize space; it would help demilitarize the arsenals of Earth. It would render nuclear weapons obsolete. We will meet with the Soviets, hoping that we can agree on a way to rid the world of the threat of nuclear destruction.

We strive for peace and security, heartened by the changes all around us. Since the turn of the century, the number of democracies in the world has grown fourfold. Human freedom is on the march, and nowhere more so than our own hemisphere. Freedom is one of the deepest and noblest aspirations of the human spirit. People, worldwide, hunger for the right of self-determination, for those inalienable rights that make for human dignity and progress.

America must remain freedom's staunchest friend, for freedom is our best ally.

And it is the world's only hope, to conquer poverty and preserve peace. Every blow we inflict against poverty will be a blow against its dark allies of oppression and war. Every victory for human freedom will be a victory for world peace.

So we go forward today, a nation still mighty in its youth and powerful in its purpose. With our alliances strengthened, with our economy leading the world to a new age of economic expansion, we look forward to a world rich in possibilities. And all this because we have worked and acted together, not as members of political parties, but as Americans.

My friends, we live in a world that is lit by lightning. So much is changing and will change, but so much endures, and transcends time.

History is a ribbon, always unfurling; history is a journey. And as we continue our journey, we think of those who traveled before us. We stand together again at the steps of this symbol of our democracy—or we would have been standing at the steps if it hadn't gotten so cold. Now we are standing inside this symbol of our democracy. Now we hear again the echoes of our past: a general falls to his knees in the hard snow of Valley Forge; a lonely president paces the darkened halls, and ponders his struggle to preserve the Union; the men of the Alamo call out encouragement to each other; a settler pushes west and sings a song, and the song echoes out forever and fills the unknowing air.

It is the American sound. It is hopeful, big-hearted, idealistic, daring, decent, and fair. That's our heritage; that is our song. We sing it still. For all our problems, our differences, we are together as of old, as we raise our voices to the God who is the Author of this most tender music. And may He continue to hold us close as we fill the world with our sound—sound in unity, affection, and love—one people under God, dedicated to the dream of freedom that He has placed in the human heart, called upon now to pass that dream on to a waiting and hopeful world.

God bless you and may God bless America.[178]

President Ronald Reagan's Address to The Forty-Second Session of the

United Nations General Assembly

New York City
September 21, 1987
Remarks as prepared for delivery.

Mr. President, Mr. Secretary-General, Ambassador Reed, honored guests, and distinguished delegates:

Let me first welcome the secretary-general back from his pilgrimage for peace in the Middle East. Hundreds of thousands have already fallen in the bloody conflict between Iran and Iraq. All men and women of goodwill pray that the carnage can soon be stopped, and we pray that the secretary-general proves to be not only a pilgrim but also the architect of a lasting peace between those two nations. Mr. Secretary-General, the United States supports you, and may God guide you in your labors ahead

Like the secretary-general, all of us here today are on a kind of pilgrimage. We come from every continent, every race, and most religions to this great hall of hope, where in the name of peace we practice diplomacy. Now, diplomacy, of course, is a subtle and nuanced craft, so much so that it's said that when one of the most wily diplomats of the nineteenth century passed away other diplomats asked, on reports of his death, "What do you suppose the old fox meant by that?"

But true statesmanship requires not merely skill but something greater, something we call vision—a grasp of the present and of the possibilities of the future. I've come here today to map out for you my own vision of the world's future, one, I believe, that in its essential elements is shared by all Americans. And I hope those who see things differently will not mind if I say that we in the United States believe that the place to look first for shape of the future is not in continental masses and sea lanes, although geography is, obviously, of great importance. Neither is it in national reserves of blood and iron or, on the other hand, of money and industrial capacity, although military and economic strength are also, of course, crucial. We begin with something that is far simpler and yet far more profound: the human heart.

All over the world today, the yearnings of the human heart are redirecting the course of international affairs, putting the lie to the myth of materialism and historical determinism. We have only to open our eyes to see the simple aspirations of ordinary people writ large on the record of our times.

Last year in the Philippines, ordinary people rekindled the spirit of democracy and restored the electoral process. Some said they had performed a miracle, and if so, a similar miracle—a transition to democracy—is taking place in the Republic of Korea. Haiti, too, is making a transition. Some despair when these new, young democracies face conflicts or challenges, but growing pains are normal in democracies. The United States had them, as has every other democracy on Earth.

In Latin America too, one can hear the voices of freedom echo from the peaks and across the plains. It is the song of ordinary people marching, not in uniforms and not in military file but, rather, one by one, in simple, everyday working clothes, marching to the polls. Ten years ago only a third of the people of Latin America and the Caribbean lived in democracies or in countries that were turning to democracy; today over 90 percent do.

But this worldwide movement to democracy is not the only way in which simple, ordinary people are leading us in this room—we who are said to be the makers of history—leading us into the future. Around the world, new businesses, new economic growth, new technologies are emerging from the workshops of ordinary people with extraordinary dreams.

Here in the United States, entrepreneurial energy—reinvigorated when we cut taxes and regulations—has fueled the current economic expansion. According to scholars at the Massachusetts Institute of Technology, three-quarters of the more than thirteen and a half million new jobs that we have created in this country since the beginning of our expansion came from businesses with fewer than one hundred employees, businesses started by ordinary people who dared to take a chance. And many of our new high technologies were first developed in the garages of fledgling entrepreneurs. Yet America is not the only, or perhaps even the best, example of the dynamism and dreams that the freeing of markets set free.

In India and China, freer markets for farmers have led to an explosion in production. In Africa, governments are rethinking their policies, and where they are allowing greater economic freedom to farmers, crop production has improved. Meanwhile, in the newly industrialized countries of the Pacific Rim, free markets in services and manufacturing as well as agriculture have led to a soaring of growth and standards of living. The ASEAN nations—Japan, Korea, and Taiwan—have created the true economic miracle of the last two decades, and in each of them, much of the magic came from ordinary people who succeeded as entrepreneurs.

In Latin America, this same lesson of free markets, greater opportunity, and growth is being studied and acted on. President Sarney of Brazil spoke for many others when he said that "private initiative is the engine of economic development. In Brazil we have learned that every time the state's penetration in the economy increases, our liberty decreases." Yes, policies that release to flight ordinary people's dreams are spreading around the world. From Colombia to Turkey to Indonesia, governments are cutting taxes, reviewing their regulations, and opening opportunities for initiative.

There has been much talk in the halls of this building about the right to development. But more and more the evidence is clear that development is not itself a right. It is the product of rights: the right to own property; the right to buy and sell freely; the right to contract; the right to be free of excessive taxation and regulation, of burdensome government. There have been studies that determined that countries with low tax rates have greater growth than those with high rates.

We're all familiar with the phenomenon of the underground economy. The scholar Hernando de Soto and his colleagues have examined the situation of one country, Peru, and described an economy of the poor that bypasses crushing taxation and stifling regulation. This informal economy, as the researchers call it, is the principal supplier of many goods and services and often the only ladder for upward mobility. In the capital city, it accounts for almost all public transportation and most street markets. And the researchers concluded that, thanks to the informal economy, "the poor can work, travel, and have a roof over their heads." They might have added that, by becoming underground entrepreneurs themselves or by working for them, the poor have become less poor and the nation itself richer.

Those who advocate statist solutions to development should take note: the free market is the other path to development and the one true path. And unlike many other paths, it leads somewhere. It works. So, this is where I believe we can find the map to the world's future: in the hearts of ordinary people, in their hopes for themselves and their children, in their prayers as they lay themselves and their families to rest each night. These simple people are the giants of the earth, the true builders of the world and shapers of the centuries to come. And if indeed they triumph, as I believe they will, we will at last know a world of peace and freedom, opportunity and hope, and, yes, of democracy—a world in which the spirit of mankind at last conquers the old, familiar enemies of famine, disease, tyranny, and war.

This is my vision—America's vision. I recognize that some governments represented in this hall have other ideas. Some do not believe in democracy or in political, economic, or religious freedom. Some believe in dictatorship, whether by one man, one party, one class, one race, or one vanguard. To those governments I would only say that the price of oppression is clear. Your economies will fall farther and farther behind. Your people will become more restless. Isn't it better to listen to the people's hopes now rather than their curses later?

And yet despite our differences, there is one common hope that brought us all to make this common pilgrimage: the hope that mankind will one day beat its swords into plowshares, the hope of peace. In no place on Earth today is peace more in need of friends than the Middle East. Its people's yearning for peace is growing. The United States will continue to be an active partner in the efforts of the parties to come together to settle their differences and build a just and lasting peace.

And this month marks the beginning of the eighth year of the Iran-Iraq War. Two months ago, the Security Council adopted a mandatory resolution demanding a ceasefire, withdrawal, and negotiations to end the war. The United States fully supports implementation of Resolution 598, as we support the secretary-general's recent mission. We welcomed Iraq's acceptance of that resolution and remain disappointed at Iran's unwillingness to accept it. In that regard, I know that the president of Iran will be addressing you tomorrow. I take this opportunity to call upon him clearly and unequivocally to state whether Iran accepts 598 or not. If the answer is positive, it would be a welcome step and major breakthrough. If it is negative, the council has no choice but rapidly to adopt enforcement measures.

For forty years the United States has made it clear, its vital interest in the security of the Persian Gulf and the countries that border it. The oil reserves there are of strategic importance to the economies of the free world. We're committed to maintaining the free flow of this oil and to preventing the domination of the region by any hostile power. We do not seek confrontation or trouble with Iran or anyone else. Our object is—or, objective is now, and has been at every stage, finding a means to end the war with no victor and no vanquished. The increase in our naval presence in the gulf does not favor one side or the other. It is a response to heightened tensions and followed consultations with our friends in the region. When the tension diminishes, so will our presence.

The United States is gratified by many recent diplomatic developments: the unanimous adoption of Resolution 598, the Arab League's statement at its recent meeting in Tunis, and the secretary-general's visit. Yet problems remain.

The Soviet Union helped in drafting and reaching an agreement on Resolution 598, but outside the Security Council, the Soviets have acted differently. They called for removal of our Navy from the gulf, where it has been for forty years. They made the false accusation that somehow the United States, rather than the war itself, is the source of tension in the gulf. Well, such statements are not helpful. They divert attention from the challenge facing us all: a just end to the war. The United States hopes the Soviets will join the other members of the Security Council in vigorously seeking an end to a conflict that never should have begun, should have ended long ago, and has become one of the great tragedies of the postwar era.

Elsewhere in the region, we see the continuing Soviet occupation of Afghanistan. After nearly eight years, a million casualties, nearly four million others driven into exile, and more intense fighting than ever, it's time for the Soviet Union to leave. The Afghan people must have the right to determine their own future free of foreign coercion. There is no excuse for prolonging a brutal war or propping up a regime whose days are clearly numbered. That regime offers political proposals that pretend compromise, but really would ensure the perpetuation of the regime's power. Those proposals have failed the only significant test: they have been rejected by the Afghan people.

Every day the resistance grows in strength. It is an indispensable party in the quest for a negotiated solution.

The world community must continue to insist on genuine self-determination, prompt and full Soviet withdrawal, and the return of the refugees to their homes in safety and honor. The attempt may be made to pressure a few countries to change their vote this year, but this body, I know, will vote overwhelmingly, as every year before, for Afghan independence and freedom. We have noted General Secretary Gorbachev's statement of readiness to withdraw. In April I asked the Soviet Union to set a date this year when this withdrawal would begin. I repeat that request now in this forum for peace. I pledge that, once the Soviet Union shows convincingly that it's ready for a genuine political settlement, the United States is ready to be helpful.

Let me add one final note on this matter. Pakistan, in the face of enormous pressure and intimidation, has given sanctuary to Afghan refugees. We salute the courage of Pakistan and the Pakistani people. They deserve strong support from all of us.

Another regional conflict, we all know, is taking place in Central America, in Nicaragua. To the Sandinista delegation here today I say: your people know the true nature of your regime. They have seen their liberties suppressed. They have seen the promises of 1979 go unfulfilled. They have seen their real wages and personal income fall by half—yes, half—since 1979, while your party elite live lives of privilege and luxury. This is why, despite a billion dollars in Soviet-bloc aid last year alone, despite the largest and best equipped army in Central America, you face a popular revolution at home. It is why the democratic resistance is able to operate freely deep in your heartland. But this revolution should come as no surprise to you; it is only the revolution you promised the people and that you then betrayed.

The goal of United States policy toward Nicaragua is simple. It is the goal of the Nicaraguan people and the freedom fighters as well. It is democracy—real, free, pluralistic, constitutional democracy. Understand this: we will not, and the world community will not, accept phony democratization designed to mask the perpetuation of dictatorship. In this two hundredth year of our own Constitution, we know that real democracy depends on the safeguards of an institutional structure that prevents a concentration of power. It is that which makes rights secure. The temporary relaxation of controls, which can later be tightened, is not democratization.

And, again, to the Sandinistas, I say: we continue to hope that Nicaragua will become part of the genuine democratic transformation that we have seen throughout Central America in this decade. We applaud the principles embodied in the Guatemala agreement, which links the security of the Central American democracies to democratic reform in Nicaragua. Now is the time for you to shut down the military machine that threatens your neighbors and assaults your own people. You must end your stranglehold on internal political activity. You must hold free and fair national elections. The media must be truly free, not censored or intimidated or crippled by indirect measures, like the denial of newsprint or threats against journalists or their families. Exiles must be allowed to return to minister, to live, to work, and to organize politically. Then, when persecution of religion has ended and the jails no longer contain political prisoners, national reconciliation and democracy will be possible. Unless this happens, democratization will be a fraud. And until it happens, we will press for true democracy by supporting those fighting for it.

Freedom in Nicaragua or Angola or Afghanistan or Cambodia or Eastern Europe or South Africa or anyplace else on the globe is not just an internal matter. Some time ago the Czech dissident writer Vaclav Havel warned the world that "respect for human rights is the fundamental condition and the sole genuine guarantee of true peace." And Andrei Sakharov in his Nobel lecture said: "I am convinced that international confidence, mutual understanding, disarmament, and international security are inconceivable without an open society with freedom of information, freedom of conscience, the right to publish, and the right to travel and choose the country in which one wishes to live." Freedom serves peace; the quest for peace must serve the cause of freedom. Patient diplomacy can contribute to a world in which both can flourish.

We're heartened by new prospects for improvement in East-West and particularly U.S.-Soviet relations. Last week Soviet foreign minister Shevardnadze visited Washington for talks with me and with the secretary of state, Shultz. We discussed the full range of issues, including my longstanding efforts to achieve, for the first time, deep reductions in U.S. and Soviet nuclear arms. It was six years ago, for example, that I proposed the zero option for U.S. and Soviet longer-range, intermediate-range nuclear missiles. I'm pleased that we have now agreed in principle to a truly historic treaty that will eliminate an entire class of U.S. and Soviet nuclear weapons. We also agreed to intensify our diplomatic efforts in all areas of mutual interest. Toward that end, Secretary Shultz and the foreign minister will meet again a month from now in Moscow, and I will meet again with General Secretary Gorbachev later this fall.

We continue to have our differences and probably always will. But that puts a special responsibility on us to find ways—realistic ways—to bring greater stability to our competition and to show the world a constructive example of the value of communication and of the possibility of peaceful solutions to political problems. And here let me add that we seek, through our Strategic Defense Initiative, to find a way to keep peace through relying on defense, not offense, for deterrence and for eventually rendering ballistic missiles obsolete. SDI has greatly enhanced the prospects for real arms reduction. It is a crucial part of our efforts to ensure a safer world and a more stable strategic balance.

We will continue to pursue the goal of arms reduction, particularly the goal that the general secretary and I agreed upon: a 50 percent reduction in our respective strategic nuclear arms. We will continue to press the Soviets for more constructive conduct in the settling of regional conflicts. We look to the Soviets to honor the Helsinki accords. We look for greater freedom for the Soviet peoples within their country, more people-to-people exchanges with our country, and Soviet recognition in practice of the right of freedom of movement.

We look forward to a time when things we now regard as sources of friction and even danger can become examples of cooperation between ourselves and the Soviet Union. For instance, I have proposed a collaboration to reduce the barriers between East and West in Berlin and, more broadly, in Europe as a whole. Let us work together for a Europe in which force of the threat—or, force, whether in the form of walls or of guns, is no longer an obstacle to free choice by individuals and whole nations. I have also called for more openness in the flow of information from the Soviet Union about its military forces, policies, and programs so that our negotiations about arms reductions can proceed with greater confidence

We hear much about changes in the Soviet Union. We're intensely interested in these changes. We hear the word "*glasnost*," which is translated as "openness" in English. "Openness" is a broad term. It means the free, unfettered flow of information, ideas, and people. It means political and intellectual liberty in all its dimensions. We hope, for the sake of the peoples of the U.S.S.R., that such changes will come. And we hope, for the sake of peace, that it will include a foreign policy that respects the freedom and independence of other peoples.

No place should be better suited for discussions of peace than this hall. The first secretary-general, Trygve Lie, said of the United Nations: "With the danger of fire, and in the absence of an organized fire department, it is only common sense for the neighbors to join in setting up their own fire brigades." Joining together to drown the flames of war—this, together with a Universal Declaration of Human Rights, was the founding ideal of the United Nations. It is our continuing challenge to ensure that the UN lives up to these hopes. As the secretary-general noted some time ago, the risk of anarchy in the world has increased, because the fundamental rules of the U.N. Charter have been violated. The General Assembly has repeatedly acknowledged this with regard to the occupation of Afghanistan. The charter has a concrete practical meaning today, because it touches on all the dimensions of human aspiration that I mentioned earlier—the yearning for democracy and freedom, for global peace, and for prosperity.

This is why we must protect the Universal Declaration of Human Rights from being debased as it was through the infamous "Zionism Is Racism" resolution. We cannot permit attempts to control the media and promote censorship under the ruse of a so-called New World Information Order. We must work against efforts to introduce contentious and nonrelevant issues into the work of the specialized and technical agencies, where we seek progress on urgent problems—from terrorism to drug trafficking to nuclear proliferation—which threaten us all. Such efforts corrupt the charter and weaken this organization.

There have been important administrative and budget reforms. They have helped. The United States is committed to restoring its contribution as reforms progress. But there is still much to do. The United Nations was built on great dreams and great ideals. Sometimes it has strayed. It is time for it to come home. It was Dag Hammarskjöld who said: "The end of all political effort must be the well-being of the individual in a life of safety and freedom." Well, should this not be our credo in the years ahead?

I have spoken today of a vision and the obstacles to its realization. More than a century ago a young Frenchman, Alexis de Tocqueville, visited America. After that visit he predicted that the two great powers of the future world would be, on one hand, the United States, which would be built, as he said, "by the plowshare," and, on the other, Russia, which would go forward, again, as he said, "by the sword." Yet need it be so? Cannot swords be turned to plowshares? Can we and all nations not live in peace? In our obsession with antagonisms of the moment, we often forget how much unites all the members of humanity. Perhaps we need some outside, universal threat to make us recognize this common bond. I occasionally think how quickly our differences worldwide would vanish if we were facing an alien threat from outside this world. And yet, I ask you, is not an alien force already among us? What could be more alien to the universal aspirations of our peoples than war and the threat of war?

Two centuries ago, in a hall much smaller than this one, in Philadelphia, Americans met to draft a constitution. In the course of their debates, one of them said that the new government, if it was to rise high, must be built on the broadest base: the will and consent of the people. And so it was, and so it has been.

My message today is that the dreams of ordinary people reach to astonishing heights. If we diplomatic pilgrims are to achieve equal altitudes, we must build all we do on the full breadth of humanity's will and consent and the full expanse of the human heart. Thank you, and God bless you all.[179]

President Ronald Reagan's Address to the Nation on the Economy

February 5, 1981
Remarks as prepared for delivery.

Good evening.

I'm speaking to you tonight to give you a report on the state of our nation's economy. I regret to say that we're in the worst economic mess since the Great Depression.

---
[179]   https://www.reaganlibrary.gov/research/speeches/092187b

A few days ago I was presented with a report I'd asked for, a comprehensive audit, if you will, of our economic condition. You won't like it. I didn't like it. But we have to face the truth and then go to work to turn things around. And make no mistake about it, we can turn them around.

I'm not going to subject you to the jumble of charts, figures, and economic jargon of that audit, but rather will try to explain where we are, how we got there, and how we can get back. First, however, let me just give a few "attention getters" from the audit.

The federal budget is out of control, and we face runaway deficits of almost eighty billion dollars for this budget year that ends September 30. That deficit is larger than the entire federal budget in 1957, and so is the almost eighty billion dollars we will pay in interest this year on the national debt.

Twenty years ago, in 1960, our federal government payroll was less than thirteen billion dollars. Today it is seventy-five billion. During these twenty years our population has only increased by 23.3 percent. The federal budget has gone up 528 percent.

Now, we've just had two years of back-to-back double-digit inflation—13.3 percent in 1979, 12.4 percent last year. The last time this happened was in World War I.

In 1960 mortgage interest rates averaged about 6 percent. They're two and a half times as high now, 15.4 percent.

The percentage of your earnings the federal government took in taxes in 1960 has almost doubled.

And finally, there are seven million Americans caught up in the personal indignity and human tragedy of unemployment. If they stood in a line, allowing three feet for each person, the line would reach from the coast of Maine to California.

Well, so much for the audit itself. Let me try to put this in personal terms. Here is a dollar such as you earned, spent, or saved in 1960. And here is a quarter, a dime, and a penny—thirty-six cents. That's what this 1960 dollar is worth today. And if the present world inflation rate should continue three more years, that dollar of 1960 will be worth a quarter. What initiative is there to save? And if we don't save, we're short of the investment capital needed for business and industry expansion. Workers in Japan and West Germany save several times the percentage of their income than Americans do.

What's happened to that American dream of owning a home? Only ten years ago, a family could buy a home, and the monthly payment averaged little more than a quarter—twenty-seven cents out of each dollar earned. Today, it takes forty-two cents out of every dollar of income. So, fewer than one out of eleven families can afford to buy their first new home.

Regulations adopted by government with the best of intentions have added $666 to the cost of an automobile. It is estimated that altogether regulations of every kind, on shopkeepers, farmers, and major industries, add one hundred billion dollars or more to the cost of the goods and services we buy. And then another twenty billion is spent by government handling the paperwork created by those regulations.

I'm sure you're getting the idea that the audit presented to me found government policies of the last few decades responsible for our economic troubles. We forgot or just overlooked the fact that government—any government—has a built-in tendency to grow. Now, we all had a hand in looking to government for benefits as if government had some source of revenue other than our earnings. Many if not most of the things we thought of or that government offered to us seemed attractive.

In the years following the Second World War it was easy, for a while at least, to overlook the price tag. Our income more than doubled in the twenty-five years after the war. We increased our take-home pay in those twenty-five years by more than we had amassed in all the preceding 150 years put together. Yes, there was some inflation, one or one and a half percent a year. That didn't bother us. But if we look back at those golden years, we recall that even then voices had been raised, warning that inflation, like radioactivity, was cumulative and that once started it could get out of control.

Some government programs seemed so worthwhile that borrowing to fund them didn't bother us. By 1960 our national debt stood at $284 billion. Congress in 1971 decided to put a ceiling of 400 billion on our ability to borrow. Today the debt is 934 billion. So-called temporary increases or extensions in the debt ceiling have been allowed twenty-one times in these ten years, and now I've been forced to ask for another increase in the debt ceiling or the government will be unable to function past the middle of February—and I've only been here sixteen days. Before we reach the day when we can reduce the debt ceiling, we may in spite of our best efforts see a national debt in excess of a trillion dollars. Now, this is a figure that's literally beyond our comprehension.

We know now that inflation results from all that deficit spending. Government has only two ways of getting money other than raising taxes. It can go into the money market and borrow, competing with its own citizens and driving up interest rates, which it has done, or it can print money, and it's done that. Both methods are inflationary.

We're victims of language. The very word "inflation" leads us to think of it as just high prices. Then, of course, we resent the person who puts on the price tags, forgetting that he or she is also a victim of inflation. Inflation is not just high prices; it's a reduction in the value of our money. When the money supply is increased but the goods and services available for buying are not, we have too much money chasing too few goods. Wars are usually accompanied by inflation. Everyone is working or fighting, but production is of weapons and munitions, not things we can buy and use.

Now, one way out would be to raise taxes so that government need not borrow or print money. But in all these years of government growth, we've reached, indeed surpassed, the limit of our people's tolerance or ability to bear an increase in the tax burden. Prior to World War Two, taxes were such that on the average we only had to work just a little over one month each year to pay our total federal, state, and local tax bill. Today we have to work four months to pay that bill.

Some say shift the tax burden to business and industry, but business doesn't pay taxes. Oh, don't get the wrong idea. Business is being taxed, so much so that we're being priced out of the world market. But business must pass its costs of operations—and that includes taxes—on to the customer in the price of the product. Only people pay taxes, all the taxes. Government just uses business in a kind of sneaky way to help collect the taxes. They're hidden in the price; we aren't aware of how much tax we actually pay.

Today this once great industrial giant of ours has the lowest rate of gain in productivity of virtually all the industrial nations with whom we must compete in the world market. We can't even hold our own market here in America against foreign automobiles, steel, and a number of other products. Japanese production of automobiles is almost twice as great per worker as it is in America. Japanese steelworkers outproduce their American counterparts by about 25 percent.

Now, this isn't because they're better workers. I'll match the American working man or woman against anyone in the world. But we have to give them the tools and equipment that workers in the other industrial nations have.

We invented the assembly line and mass production, but punitive tax policies and excessive and unnecessary regulations plus government borrowing have stifled our ability to update plant and equipment. When capital investment is made, it's too often for some unproductive alterations demanded by government to meet various of its regulations. Excessive taxation of individuals has robbed us of incentive and made overtime unprofitable.

We once produced about 40 percent of the world's steel. We now produce 19 percent. We were once the greatest producer of automobiles, producing more than all the rest of the world combined. That is no longer true, and in addition, the "Big Three," the major auto companies in our land, have sustained tremendous losses in the past year and have been forced to lay off thousands of workers.

All of you who are working know that even with cost-of-living pay raises, you can't keep up with inflation. In our progressive tax system, as you increase the number of dollars you earn, you find yourself moved up into higher tax brackets, paying a higher tax rate just for trying to hold your own. The result? Your standard of living is going down.

Over the past decades, we've talked of curtailing government spending so that we can then lower the tax burden. Sometimes we've even taken a run at doing that. But there were always those who told us that taxes couldn't be cut until spending was reduced. Well, you know, we can lecture our children about extravagance until we run out of voice and breath. Or we can cure their extravagance by simply reducing their allowance.

It's time to recognize that we've come to a turning point. We're threatened with an economic calamity of tremendous proportions, and the old business-as-usual treatment can't save us. Together, we must chart a different course.

We must increase productivity. That means making it possible for industry to modernize and make use of the technology which we ourselves invented. That means putting Americans back to work. And that means above all bringing government spending back within government revenues, which is the only way, together with increased productivity, that we can reduce and, yes, eliminate inflation.

In the past we've tried to fight inflation one year and then, with unemployment increased, turn the next year to fighting unemployment with more deficit spending as a pump primer. So, again, up goes inflation. It hasn't worked. We don't have to choose between inflation and unemployment—they go hand in hand. It's time to try something different, and that's what we're going to do.

I've already placed a freeze on hiring replacements for those who retire or leave government service. I've ordered a cut in government travel, the number of consultants to the government, and the buying of office equipment and other items. I've put a freeze on pending regulations and set up a task force under Vice President Bush to review regulations with an eye toward getting rid of as many as possible. I have decontrolled oil, which should result in more domestic production and less dependence on foreign oil. And I'm eliminating that ineffective Council on Wage and Price Stability.

But it will take more, much more. And we must realize there is no quick fix. At the same time, however, we cannot delay in implementing an economic program aimed at both reducing tax rates to stimulate productivity and reducing the growth in government spending to reduce unemployment and inflation.

On February 18, I will present in detail an economic program to Congress embodying the features I've just stated. It will propose budget cuts in virtually every department of government. It is my belief that these actual budget cuts will only be part of the savings. As our Cabinet secretaries take charge of their departments, they will search out areas of waste, extravagance, and costly overhead which could yield additional and substantial reductions.

Now, at the same time we're doing this, we must go forward with a tax relief package. I shall ask for a 10 percent reduction across the board in personal income tax rates for each of the next three years. Proposals will also be submitted for accelerated depreciation allowances for business to provide necessary capital so as to create jobs.

Now, here again, in saying this, I know that language, as I said earlier, can get in the way of a clear understanding of what our program is intended to do. Budget cuts can sound as if we're going to reduce total government spending to a lower level than was spent the year before. Well, this is not the case. The budgets will increase as our population increases, and each year we'll see spending increases to match that growth. Government revenues will increase as the economy grows, but the burden will be lighter for each individual, because the economic base will have been expanded by reason of the reduced rates.

Now, let me show you a chart that I've had drawn to illustrate how this can be.

Here you see two trend lines. The bottom line shows the increase in tax revenues. The red line on top is the increase in government spending. Both lines turn upward, reflecting the giant tax increase already built into the system for this year 1981, and the increases in spending built into the '81 and '82 budgets and on into the future. As you can see, the spending line rises at a steeper slant than the revenue line. And that gap between those lines illustrates the increasing deficits we've been running, including this year's eighty-billion-dollar deficit.

Now, in the second chart, the lines represent the positive effects when Congress accepts our economic program. Both lines continue to rise, allowing for necessary growth, but the gap narrows as spending cuts continue over the next few years until finally the two lines come together, meaning a balanced budget.

I am confident that my administration can achieve that. At that point tax revenues, in spite of rate reductions, will be increasing faster than spending, which means we can look forward to further reductions in the tax rates.

Now, in all of this we will, of course, work closely with the Federal Reserve System toward the objective of a stable monetary policy.

Our spending cuts will not be at the expense of the truly needy. We will, however, seek to eliminate benefits to those who are not really qualified by reason of need.

As I've said before, on February 18 I will present this economic package of budget reductions and tax reform to a joint session of Congress and to you in full detail.

Our basic system is sound. We can, with compassion, continue to meet our responsibility to those who, through no fault of their own, need our help. We can meet fully the other legitimate responsibilities of government. We cannot continue any longer our wasteful ways at the expense of the workers of this land or of our children.

Since 1960 our government has spent $5.1 trillion. Our debt has grown by 648 billion. Prices have exploded by 178 percent. How much better off are we for all that? Well, we all know we're very much worse off. When we measure how harshly these years of inflation, lower productivity, and uncontrolled government growth have affected our lives, we know we must act and act now. We must not be timid. We will restore the freedom of all men and women to excel and to create. We will unleash the energy and genius of the American people, traits which have never failed us.

To the Congress of the United States, I extend my hand in cooperation, and I believe we can go forward in a bipartisan manner. I've found a real willingness to cooperate on the part of Democrats and members of my own party.

To my colleagues in the executive branch of government and to all federal employees, I ask that we work in the spirit of service.

I urge those great institutions in America, business and labor, to be guided by the national interest, and I'm confident they will. The only special interest that we will serve is the interest of all the people.

We can create the incentives which take advantage of the genius of our economic system—a system, as Walter Lippmann observed more than forty years ago, which for the first time in history gave men "a way of producing wealth in which the good fortune of others multiplied their own."

Our aim is to increase our national wealth so all will have more, not just redistribute what we already have, which is just a sharing of scarcity. We can begin to reward hard work and risk-taking, by forcing this government to live within its means.

Over the years, we've let negative economic forces run out of control. We stalled the judgment day, but we no longer have that luxury. We're out of time.

And to you, my fellow citizens, let us join in a new determination to rebuild the foundation of our society, to work together, to act responsibly. Let us do so with the most profound respect for that which must be preserved as well as with sensitive understanding and compassion for those who must be protected.

We can leave our children with an unrepayable massive debt and a shattered economy, or we can leave them liberty in a land where every individual has the opportunity to be whatever God intended us to be. All it takes is a little common sense and recognition of our own ability. Together we can forge a new beginning for America.

Thank you, and goodnight.[180]

President Ronald Reagan's Remarks at a Ceremony Commemorating the Fortieth Anniversary of the Normandy Invasion, D-Day

Normandy, France
June 6, 1984
Remarks as prepared for delivery.

We're here to mark that day in history when the Allied armies joined in battle to reclaim this continent to liberty. For four long years, much of Europe had been under a terrible shadow. Free nations had fallen, Jews cried out in the camps, millions cried out for liberation. Europe was enslaved, and the world prayed for its rescue. Here in Normandy the rescue began. Here the Allies stood and fought against tyranny in a giant undertaking unparalleled in human history.

We stand on a lonely, windswept point on the northern shore of France. The air is soft, but forty years ago at this moment, the air was dense with smoke and the cries of men, and the air was filled with the crack of rifle fire and the roar of cannon. At dawn, on the morning of the sixth of June, 1944, 225 Rangers jumped off the British landing craft and ran to the bottom of these cliffs.

Their mission was one of the most difficult and daring of the invasion: to climb these sheer and desolate cliffs and take

---

[180]   https://www.reaganlibrary.gov/research/speeches/20581c

out the enemy guns. The Allies had been told that some of the mightiest of these guns were here and they would be trained on the beaches to stop the Allied advance. The Rangers looked up and saw the enemy soldiers—the edge of the cliffs shooting down at them with machine guns and throwing grenades. And the American Rangers began to climb. They shot rope ladders over the face of these cliffs and began to pull themselves up. When one Ranger fell, another would take his place. When one rope was cut, a Ranger would grab another and begin his climb again. They climbed, shot back, and held their footing. Soon, one by one, the Rangers pulled themselves over the top, and in seizing the firm land at the top of these cliffs, they began to seize back the continent of Europe. Two hundred and twenty-five came here. After two days of fighting, only ninety could still bear arms.

Behind me is a memorial that symbolizes the Ranger daggers that were thrust into the top of these cliffs. And before me are the men who put them there. These are the boys of Pointe du Hoc. These are the men who took the cliffs. These are the champions who helped free a continent. These are the heroes who helped end a war. Gentlemen, I look at you and I think of the words of Stephen Spender's poem. You are men who in your "lives fought for life...and left the vivid air signed with your honor." I think I know what you may be thinking right now—thinking, "We were just part of a bigger effort; everyone was brave that day." Well, everyone was. Do you remember the story of Bill Millin of the Fifty-First Highlanders? Forty years ago today, British troops were pinned down near a bridge, waiting desperately for help. Suddenly, they heard the sound of bagpipes, and some thought they were dreaming. Well, they weren't.

They looked up and saw Bill Millin with his bagpipes, leading the reinforcements and ignoring the smack of the bullets into the ground around him. Lord Lovat was with him—Lord Lovat of Scotland, who calmly announced when he got to the bridge, "Sorry I'm a few minutes late," as if he'd been delayed by a traffic jam, when in truth he'd just come from the bloody fighting on Sword Beach, which he and his men had just taken. There was the impossible valor of the Poles who threw themselves between the enemy and the rest of Europe as the invasion took hold, and the unsurpassed courage of the Canadians who had already seen the horrors of war on this coast. They knew what awaited them there, but they would not be deterred. And once they hit Juno Beach, they never looked back. All of these men were part of a roll call of honor with names that spoke of a pride as bright as the colors they bore: the Royal Winnipeg Rifles, Poland's Twenty-Fourth Lancers, the Royal Scots Fusiliers, the Screaming Eagles, the Yeomen of England's armored divisions, the forces of Free France, the Coast Guard's "Matchbox Fleet" and you, the American Rangers. Forty summers have passed since the battle that you fought here. You were young the day you took these cliffs; some of you were hardly more than boys, with the deepest joys of life before you. Yet, you risked everything here. Why? Why did you do it? What impelled you to put aside the instinct for self-preservation and risk your lives to take these cliffs? What inspired all the men of the armies that met here? We look at you, and somehow we know the answer. It was faith and belief; it was loyalty and love.

The men of Normandy had faith that what they were doing was right, faith that they fought for all humanity, faith that a just God would grant them mercy on this beachhead or on the next. It was the deep knowledge—and pray God we have not lost it—that there is a profound, moral difference between the use of force for liberation and the use of force for conquest. You were here to liberate, not to conquer, and so you and those others did not doubt your cause. And you were right not to doubt. You all knew that some things are worth dying for. One's country is worth dying for, and democracy is worth dying for, because it's the most deeply honorable form of government ever devised by man. All of you loved liberty. All of you were willing to fight tyranny, and you knew the people of your countries were behind you.

The Americans who fought here that morning knew word of the invasion was spreading through the darkness back home. They fought—or felt in their hearts, though they couldn't know in fact, that in Georgia they were filling the churches at four a.m., in Kansas they were kneeling on their porches and praying, and in Philadelphia they were ringing the Liberty Bell. Something else helped the men of D-Day: their rock-hard belief that Providence would have a great hand in the events that would unfold here; that God was an ally in this great cause. And so, the night before the invasion, when Colonel Wolverton asked his parachute troops to kneel with him in prayer he told them: "Do not bow your heads, but look up so you can see God and ask His blessing in what we're about to do." Also that night, General Matthew Ridgway on his cot, listening in the darkness for the promise God made to Joshua: "I will not fail thee nor forsake thee." These are the things that impelled them; these are the things that shaped the unity of the Allies.

When the war was over, there were lives to be rebuilt and governments to be returned to the people. There were nations to be reborn. Above all, there was a new peace to be assured. These were huge and daunting tasks. But the Allies summoned strength from the faith, belief, loyalty, and love of those who fell here. They rebuilt a new Europe together. There was first a great reconciliation among those who had been enemies, all of whom had suffered so greatly.

The United States did its part, creating the Marshall Plan to help rebuild our allies and our former enemies. The Marshall Plan led to the Atlantic alliance—a great alliance that serves to this day as our shield for freedom, for prosperity, and for peace. In spite of our great efforts and successes, not all that followed the end of the war was happy or planned. Some liberated countries were lost. The great sadness of this loss echoes down to our own time in the streets of Warsaw, Prague, and East Berlin. Soviet troops that came to the center of this continent did not leave when peace came. They're still there, uninvited, unwanted, unyielding, almost forty years after the war. Because of this, Allied forces still stand on this continent. Today, as forty years ago, our armies are here for only one purpose—to protect and defend democracy. The only territories we hold are memorials like this one and graveyards where our heroes rest.

We in America have learned bitter lessons from two World Wars: it is better to be here ready to protect the peace than to take blind shelter across the sea, rushing to respond only after freedom is lost. We've learned that isolationism never was and never will be an acceptable response to tyrannical governments with an expansionist intent. But we try always to be prepared for peace; prepared to deter aggression; prepared to negotiate the reduction of arms; and, yes, prepared to reach out again in the spirit of reconciliation. In truth, there is no reconciliation we would welcome more than a reconciliation with the Soviet Union, so, together, we can lessen the risks of war, now and forever.

It's fitting to remember here the great losses also suffered by the Russian people during World War Two: twenty million perished, a terrible price that testifies to all the world the necessity of ending war. I tell you from my heart that we in the United States do not want war. We want to wipe from the face of the earth the terrible weapons that man now has in his hands. And I tell you, we are ready to seize that beachhead. We look for some sign from the Soviet Union that they are willing to move forward, that they share our desire and love for peace, and that they will give up the ways of conquest.

There must be a changing there that will allow us to turn our hope into action. We will pray forever that someday that changing will come. But for now, particularly today, it is good and fitting to renew our commitment to each other, to our freedom, and to the alliance that protects it. We are bound today by what bound us forty years ago, the same loyalties, traditions, and beliefs. We're bound by reality. The strength of America's allies is vital to the United States, and the American security guarantee is essential to the continued freedom of Europe's democracies. We were with you then; we are with you now. Your hopes are our hopes, and your destiny is our destiny. Here, in this place where the West held together, let us make a vow to our dead. Let us show them by our actions that we understand what they died for. Let our actions say to them the words for which Matthew Ridgway listened: "I will not fail thee nor forsake thee." Strengthened by their courage, heartened by their valor, and borne by their memory, let us continue to stand for the ideals for which they lived and died. Thank you very much, and God bless you all.[181]

---

[181]   https://www.reaganfoundation.org/media/128809/normandy.pdf